INDIANA TRIVIA

INDIANA TRIVIA

**COMPILED BY
ERNIE & JILL COUCH**

Rutledge Hill Press
Nashville, Tennessee

Published by Rutledge Hill Press, Inc., 513 Third Avenue
South, Nashville, Tennessee 37210

Typography by Bailey Typography, Inc.
Cover photography by Doug Brachey Photography
Color separation by Manning Camera Graphics
Book and cover design by Ernie Couch/Consultx

Printed in the United States of America
1 2 3 4 5 6 7 8 — 93 92 91 90 89

PREFACE

Indiana is comprised of a richly diversified land and people with colorful traditions and a compelling history. Captured within these pages are some of the highlights of this rich Hoosier heritage, both the known and not-so-well-known.

Indiana Trivia is designed to be informative, educational, and entertaining. But most of all we hope that you will be motivated to learn more about the great state of Indiana.

—Ernie & Jill Couch

To
Ron Mathis
and
the great people of Indiana

TABLE OF CONTENTS

GEOGRAPHY

C H A P T E R   O N E

Q. What Dearborn County town was named by Judge Jesse Holman in 1819 for the Roman goddess of the dawn?

A. Aurora.

———◆———

Q. Near what Indiana city did Johnny Appleseed die in 1845?

A. Fort Wayne.

———◆———

Q. What two adjoining Indiana counties contain communities named Pumpkin Center?

A. Orange and Washington.

———◆———

Q. In what Indiana city on October 1, 1842 was Henry Clay publicly presented with a petition, signed by 2,000 local Quakers, calling for him to free his slaves?

A. Richmond.

———◆———

Q. Where was Vice President Dan Quayle born on February 4, 1947?

A. Indianapolis.

Q. Where in 1807 did the Robertson Methodist Society, build the first Methodist church in Indiana?

A. Charlestown.

———◆———

Q. What Indiana city was laid out and named in 1802 by William Henry Harrison?

A. Jeffersonville.

———◆———

Q. The community of Gnaw Bone is situated in what county?

A. Brown.

———◆———

Q. What Indiana city, settled in 1815, received its name from observations made by pioneers of blooming wildflowers?

A. Bloomington.

———◆———

Q. Prior to 1877, what was the seat of Clay County?

A. Bowling Green.

———◆———

Q. What Lawrence County town is named for a construction engineer on the Ohio & Mississippi Railroad who later became a Union Army general?

A. Mitchell.

———◆———

Q. Jasper is the seat of what county?

A. Dubois.

Q. What is the meaning of the French place-name Terre Haute?

A. "High land."

———◆———

Q. Noted Socialist and labor leader Eugene V. Debs was born in what Indiana city in 1855?

A. Terre Haute.

———◆———

Q. What is the oldest town in Indiana?

A. Vincennes.

———◆———

Q. Where did Dr. J. Westerfield from Anderson found a Spiritualist camp in 1890?

A. Chesterfield.

———◆———

Q. What was the first permanent white settlement in Washington County?

A. Becks Mill.

———◆———

Q. General Andrew Jackson's famous victory over the British in Louisiana led to the naming of what Orange County town?

A. Orleans.

———◆———

Q. What was the last Indiana town to be raided by Confederate General John Hunt Morgan and his troops?

A. West Harrison.

Q. What community founded in 1837 serves as the seat of Perry County?

A. Cannelton.

———◆———

Q. Prior to 1818, what was the seat of Perry County?

A. Troy.

———◆———

Q. By what name was the site of Grandview known to the Indians?

A. Weesoe Wasapinuk ("yellow tree and bank of big water").

———◆———

Q. During the late 1800s, what two western Orange County communities were the site of some of the nation's most fashionable resorts?

A. West Baden Springs and French Lick.

———◆———

Q. On the site of what present-day Indiana city was the Treaty of Paradise Springs signed in October 1826?

A. Wabash.

———◆———

Q. Where was the first normal school in Indiana opened by Isaac Mahurin in 1852?

A. Burnettsville.

———◆———

Q. By what name was Crown Point first called?

A. Robinson's Prairie.

Q. What was the first road through Randolph County?

A. Quaker Trace.

———————◆———————

Q. Near what Franklin County town was the first Baptist church in Indiana, the Little Cedar Baptist Church, erected in 1812?

A. Brookville.

———————◆———————

Q. What four states border Indiana?

A. Michigan, Ohio, Kentucky, and Illinois.

———————◆———————

Q. "Keep knee deep in mud," is the meaning of what LaPorte County Indian place-name?

A. Wanatah.

———————◆———————

Q. What Fort Wayne suburb was named by early settlers for a Connecticut city?

A. New Haven.

———————◆———————

Q. Prior to 1847, what Indiana town was the home of ardent abolitionist Levi Coffin?

A. Fountain City.

———————◆———————

Q. General Ambrose Burnside, who served as governor of Rhode Island for three terms, spent his childhood and teenage years in what Indiana town?

A. Liberty.

Q. Measuring forty feet in diameter, where in Indiana may the world's second largest clock be found?

A. Jeffersonville.

———◆———

Q. Grissom Air Force Base is in what Indiana county?

A. Miami.

———◆———

Q. What Indiana town has been called the "City of Firsts"?

A. Kokomo.

———◆———

Q. From 1816 to 1825, what town served as the capital of the state of Indiana?

A. Corydon.

———◆———

Q. The Tippecanoe Battlefield State Memorial is near what community?

A. Battle Ground.

———◆———

Q. Prior to 1843, what was the name of Floyds Knobs?

A. Mooresville.

———◆———

Q. By what name was Galena first called?

A. Germantown.

Q. What river forms the entire southern boundary of Indiana?

A. Ohio.

———◆———

Q. Frequent misty haze floating overhead led to the naming of what Harrison County community?

A. White Cloud.

———◆———

Q. What town was the seat of Crawford County from 1843 to 1893?

A. Leavenworth.

———◆———

Q. For whom was Dale named?

A. Robert Dale Owen.

———◆———

Q. Where did Abraham Lincoln's family attend church while living in Indiana?

A. Pigeon Creek Baptist Church.

———◆———

Q. The Christmas season led to the naming of what Spencer County town?

A. Santa Claus.

———◆———

Q. Indianapolis was laid out on a wheel pattern following the design of what other city?

A. Washington, D. C.

Q. What Indiana town was established by lawyer, doctor, and surveyor William B. Laughlin?

A. Rushville.

———◆———

Q. Settlers viewing the surrounding forests caused them to apply what biblical place-name to their Boone County community?

A. Lebanon (for the Cedars of Lebanon).

———◆———

Q. By what name was the Indian village that preceded Thorntown called?

A. Keewaskee ("place of thorns").

———◆———

Q. What Tippecanoe County city was founded and named by William Digby in 1824?

A. Lafayette.

———◆———

Q. South of Terre Haute, what river forms the western boundary of the state?

A. Wabash.

———◆———

Q. From east to west, how wide is Indiana?

A. 160 miles.

———◆———

Q. What community and body of water in the extreme northeast corner of the state share the same name?

A. Clear Lake.

Q. When established in 1836, by what name was the present-day community of Hamilton called?

A. Enterprise.

———◆———

Q. Which Indiana town is the home of Tri-State University?

A. Angola.

———◆———

Q. Where in Indiana were white men first hanged for murdering Indians in 1824?

A. Pendleton.

———◆———

Q. Which Indiana town and county were named in honor of the Marquis de LaFayette's country home near Paris?

A. LaGrange.

———◆———

Q. What was the first seat of Jackson County?

A. Vallonia.

———◆———

Q. Popcorn is in the northwestern corner of what county?

A. Lawrence.

———◆———

Q. Shoals is the seventh town to serve as the seat of what county?

A. Martin.

Q. The reading of a magazine article about South America, by William Stewart led to the naming of what Clay County town?

A. Brazil.

Q. What Indianapolis suburb was laid out by Carl Fisher, James T. Allison, and Frank H. Wheeler in 1912, with the stipulation that all blacks were to be excluded as residents or proprietors?

A. Speedway City (now Speedway).

Q. DePauw University is in what Putnam County town?

A. Greencastle.

Q. Indian trader William Conner founded what Hamilton County town in 1823?

A. Noblesville.

Q. Where was Wilbur Wright born on April 16, 1867?

A. Near New Castle.

Q. For whom was Danville named?

A. Daniel Clark.

Q. What LaGrange County community and lake are named in honor of a Potawatomi Indian leader?

A. Shipshewana.

Q. In 1805 what was the first white settlement on the site of present-day Washington?

A. Fort Flora.

———◆———

Q. The beautiful sunrises over the Kentucky hills across the Ohio River led to the name of what Indiana community?

A. Rising Sun.

———◆———

Q. An Indian's interpretive description of the shape of an island at the confluence of two northern Indiana rivers led to the name of what city?

A. Elkhart.

———◆———

Q. Trail Creek flows through which Indiana city?

A. Michigan City.

———◆———

Q. In 1833 David Bundle became the first pioneer to settle on the site of what present-day Noble County town?

A. Kendallville.

———◆———

Q. The community of Wawaka derived its name from an Indian word of what meaning?

A. "Big heron."

———◆———

Q. In Parke County, what community is named for an Aztec emperor?

A. Montezuma.

Q. What northern Kosciusko County community and lake are named for an Indian chief whose nickname was "Old Fat Belly"?

A. Wawasee.

———◆———

Q. The western Indianapolis suburb of Clermont was given what name when platted in 1849?

A. Mechanicsburg.

———◆———

Q. What Montgomery County city is named in honor of a famous Indian fighter from Virginia?

A. Crawfordsville (for Colonel William Crawford).

———◆———

Q. By what Indian name was Huntington first called?

A. Wepecheange ("place of flints").

———◆———

Q. What LaGrange County community received its present name in 1884 in honor of a local military school?

A. Howe.

———◆———

Q. What Wabash County town derived its name from the corruption of an Indian chief's name?

A. Lagro (Les Gros).

———◆———

Q. With a population of over 5,000, what was the largest city in Indiana in 1850?

A. Madison.

Q. What Indiana town received its name because it is on one of the higher elevations in Henry County?

A. Mount Summit.

———◆———

Q. Prior to August 14, 1873, what was the seat of Wayne County?

A. Centerville.

———◆———

Q. What Hamilton County community is named for a Delaware Indian chief?

A. Strawtown (for Chief Straw).

———◆———

Q. US highway 40 follows what pioneer highway?

A. The National Road.

———◆———

Q. What Parke County community received its name for being situated near a campsite of General William Henry Harrison's troops?

A. Armiesburg.

———◆———

Q. What Henry County town is named for a government engineer who served in the construction of the National Road?

A. Knightstown (for John Knight).

———◆———

Q. By what name was Mount Vernon first known?

A. McFadden's Landing.

Q. What Indiana city takes its name from the English name of Delaware Indian Chief Kikthawenund?

A. Anderson (for Captain Anderson).

———◆———

Q. For whom was Princeton named?

A. Captain William Prince.

———◆———

Q. In 1841 Father Edward Sorin, later the founder of Notre Dame, seriously considered what Daviess County town as a site for a Catholic university?

A. Montgomery.

———◆———

Q. What is the smallest county in Indiana?

A. Ohio.

———◆———

Q. Where was the first state prison in Indiana established in 1821?

A. Jeffersonville.

———◆———

Q. What Gibson County town is said to be named for a worker on the Wabash and Erie Canal?

A. Francisco.

———◆———

Q. Thomas Riley Marshall, who served as vice president of the United States from 1913 to 1921, was born in what Indiana town?

A. North Manchester.

Q. What Indiana city was established where the St. Joseph and St. Mary's rivers flow together to form the Maumee River?

A. Fort Wayne.

◆

Q. Tell City is named in honor of what legendary hero?

A. William Tell.

◆

Q. What town serves as the seat of Spencer County?

A. Rockport.

◆

Q. On the site of what present-day community was the first Quaker meeting held in Indiana in 1807?

A. Richmond.

◆

Q. What four present-day states were formerly a part of the Indiana Territory?

A. Illinois, Michigan, Wisconsin, and Indiana.

◆

Q. The Howard County Historical Museum is housed in the Seiberling Mansion in what city?

A. Kokomo.

◆

Q. What Indiana city is named for the daughter of Shawnee Chief Elkhart?

A. Mishawaka.

Q. What town served as the seat of Clark County from 1811 until 1878?

A. Charlestown.

Q. When founded in 1846, what was the first proposed name for the community finally named Santa Claus?

A. Santa Fe.

Q. What was the treaty grounds of the Miami Indians near Huntington?

A. Forks of the Wabash.

Q. Where is the 1874, sixteen-room home of President Benjamin Harrison situated?

A. Indianapolis.

Q. What Catholic college, founded in 1840, is situated at St. Marys in Vigo County?

A. St. Mary-of-the-Woods College.

Q. The commuinty of Cyclone is in what county?

A. Clinton.

Q. What is the largest town in Jennings County?

A. North Vernon.

Q. What Clay County town received a fountain, the *Chafariz dos Contas,* as a gift from a South American government?

A. Brazil.

Q. How many Indiana counties are in the Central Time Zone?

A. Eleven.

Q. What is the most northeastern county in Indiana?

A. Steuben.

Q. In the past, Auburn, Cord, McFarian, and Lexington automobiles were all manufactured in what Fayette County city?

A. Connersville.

Q. Where, on July 9, 1863, was the only Civil War battle on Indiana soil fought?

A. Corydon.

Q. What town has been called the "Athens of the Hoosier State"?

A. Crawfordsville.

Q. In whose honor was Gary named?

A. Judge Elbert H. Gary.

Q. What Indiana city is the home of Ball State University?

A. Muncie.

———◆———

Q. The central portion of what county has been called "Log Cabin Country" due to the large number of historic log cabins in the area?

A. Brown.

———◆———

Q. What city is the capital of Indiana?

A. Indianapolis.

———◆———

Q. William Hayden English, onetime candidate for vice president of the United States and secretary of the State Constitutional Convention of 1850, was a native of what county?

A. Scott.

———◆———

Q. What Indiana city was laid out according to plans by Thomas Jefferson?

A. Jeffersonville.

———◆———

Q. At what Indiana town was the first Greek lettered college sorority founded on January 27, 1870?

A. Greencastle (Kappa Alpha Theta).

———◆———

Q. Both Mexico and Peru are in what county?

A. Miami.

Q. The University of Southern Indiana is in what south-eastern Indiana city.

A. Evansville.

———◆———

Q. How many counties are in Indiana?

A. Ninety-two.

———◆———

Q. What Martin County town received its name as a corruption of the names of the engineer on the first locomotive through the town and of the original landowner of the town site?

A. Loogootee (for Lowe and Gootee).

———◆———

Q. For whom is Fort Wayne named?

A. General ("Mad") Anthony Wayne.

———◆———

Q. What is the second oldest town in Floyd County?

A. Greenville.

———◆———

Q. Where in Indiana did Scottish philanthropist, industrialist, and social reformer Robert Owen attempt to establish a "perfect society" in 1825?

A. New Harmony.

———◆———

Q. What Indiana town is named in honor of the first governor of Kentucky?

A. Shelbyville (for Isaac Shelby).

Q. When Benton was founded, what Potawatomi village existed in the vicinity of the settlement?

A. Aubenaube.

———————◆———————

Q. What Whitley County town received its name from the site of a battle during the Mexican War?

A. Churubusco.

———————◆———————

Q. Early settlers finding thousands of wild rose bushes growing in the area led to the naming of what St. Joseph town?

A. Roseland.

———————◆———————

Q. Schuyler Colfax, who served as vice president of the United States under the Grant administration, named what Marshall County town?

A. Argos.

———————◆———————

Q. Founded in 1831, what town serves as the seat of Fulton County?

A. Rochester.

———————◆———————

Q. What is the largest United States city founded during the twentieth century?

A. Gary.

———————◆———————

Q. Founded in 1784, for whom is Clarksville named?

A. George Rogers Clark.

Q. What college, dating back to 1833, is in Crawfordsville?

A. Wabash College.

———◆———

Q. Historic Lockerbie Square, consisting of late nineteenth-century homes, is in what Indiana city?

A. Indianapolis.

———◆———

Q. What southern Washington County town was settled in 1805?

A. Fredericksburg.

———◆———

Q. In what county was the Lick Creek Friends Church built in 1815?

A. Orange.

———◆———

Q. What Jefferson County town is named in honor of a former United States president?

A. Madison.

———◆———

Q. Jonathan Jennings, who served as the first governor of Indiana, is buried in what community?

A. Charlestown.

———◆———

Q. John Hay, who served as Abraham Lincoln's secretary and as secretary of state in both William McKinley's and Theodore Roosevelt's administrations, was born in what Indiana town?

A. Salem.

Q. In what county does Indiana have its own Bunker Hill?

A. Miami.

◆

Q. What eastern Indiana city was known for many years as the "Rose City"?

A. New Castle.

◆

Q. The nation's first railroad apprentice school was established in what Indiana city in 1872?

A. Elkhart.

◆

Q. Where was Indiana's first women's prison managed exclusively by women opened on October 8, 1873?

A. Indianapolis.

◆

Q. Hillforest, an Italian Renaissance villa built by Thomas Gaff around 1856, may be seen in what Indiana town?

A. Aurora.

◆

Q. Where is Whitewater Canal State Historic Site?

A. Metamore.

◆

Q. In what city are the headquarters of Hoosier National Forest and Wayne National Forest situated?

A. Bedford.

Q. Outstanding architectural designs have attracted international attention to what Indiana city?

A. Columbus.

———◆———

Q. What is the seat of Warrick County?

A. Boonville.

———◆———

Q. The nineteenth-century Greek Revival-style home of former Indiana govenor Henry S. Lane may be seen in what town?

A. Crawfordsville.

———◆———

Q. In what three Indiana counties are communities named Needmore found?

A. Vermillion, Brown, and Lawrence.

———◆———

Q. What northwestern Vigo County community was named for a local coal mine owner?

A. Shirkieville.

———◆———

Q. The lake for which the community of Pleasant Lake was named was known by what name to the Indians?

A. Nipcondish ("pleasant waters").

———◆———

Q. What is the oldest town in DeKalb County?

A. Auburn.

Q. Founded in 1846, Concordia Theological Seminary, is in what Indiana city?

A. Fort Wayne.

———◆———

Q. Paoli is the seat of what county?

A. Orange.

———◆———

Q. What Adams County town was named for a naval hero?

A. Decatur (for Stephen Decatur).

———◆———

Q. Where was the first courthouse and jail of Noble County erected?

A. Augusta (two miles west of Albion).

———◆———

Q. A postmaster's unusually tall adopted daughter, Mary, provided the inspiration for the naming of what Sullivan County town?

A. Hymera (shortened from High Mary).

———◆———

Q. Where was Wendell L. Willkie born in 1892?

A. Elwood.

———◆———

Q. What fort that existed on the present-day site of Goshen provided protection for early settlers of the area?

A. Fort Beane.

Q. The community of Howe was platted in 1834 on the site of what former Potawatomi village?

A. Mongoquinong ("white squaw").

———◆———

Q. What Adams County town was founded in 1852 by Mennonite immigrants from Switzerland?

A. Berne.

———◆———

Q. Goshen is the seat of what Indiana county?

A. Elkhart.

———◆———

Q. What town, centered on the LaGrange-Noble County line, is named for a Connecticut Yankee who brought much commerce to the early community?

A. Wolcottville (for George Wolcott).

———◆———

Q. During the Wabash and Erie Canal days, what nickname was given to Williamsport?

A. "Side Cut City."

———◆———

Q. Zachariah Cicot founded what Warren County community in 1832?

A. Independence.

———◆———

Q. Hanover College is in what Indiana city?

A. Madison.

Q. What Indiana town was known as the "grand central station" of the Underground Railroad?

A. Fountain City.

Q. At what site just west of Underwood were twenty-four settlers massacred and their bodies mutilated by Indians on September 3, 1812?

A. Pigeon Roost.

Q. What Clark County town was named for a local cement manufacturer?

A. Speed (for W. S. Speed).

Q. When platted in 1823, what name was given to Anderson?

A. Andersontown.

Q. What Elkhart County town, platted in 1832, was named for a Missouri senator?

A. Benton (for Thomas H. Benton).

Q. Quakers founded what Hamilton County town in 1834?

A. Westfield.

Q. General John Tipton, John Lindsay, and Luke Bonesteel settled the site of what present-day Indiana city?

A. Columbus.

Q. What Noble County town was platted in 1839 on the former camp site of construction workers on the dam that created Sylvan Lake?

A. Rome City.

Q. Mount Vernon is the seat of what Indiana county?

A. Posey.

Q. How many counties form the northern border of Indiana?

A. Seven.

Q. What Perry County town was laid out by Swiss settlers in 1857 to accommodate 90,000 persons?

A. Tell City.

Q. Indiana's tenth governor, Joseph

A. Wright, began practicing law at the age of twenty in what town?

Q. Near what present-day community did Henry Clay and Humphrey Marshall fight a duel in 1808?

A. Clarksville.

Q. What was the original seat of LaGrange County?

A. Howe.

Q. What Indiana city was the home of the Studebaker automobile?

A. South Bend.

———◆———

Q. Birdseye is in what county?

A. Dubois.

———◆———

Q. What Indiana city is named in honor of the American Revolution general known by the nickname, "Swamp Fox"?

A. Marion (for General Francis Marion).

———◆———

Q. LaPorte is known by what nickname?

A. "City of Bridges."

———◆———

Q. What was the name of the settlement that evolved into Columbus?

A. Tiptonia.

———◆———

Q. The Lawrence County Historical Museum is in what city?

A. Bedford.

———◆———

Q. The 149,000 acres of land given to George Roger Clark and his troops for their outstanding military service was called by what name?

A. Clark's Grant.

Q. New Castle is the seat of what Indiana county?

A. Henry.

◆

Q. What Spiritualist town was laid out during the late 1850s near the farm of William Chamness, in southeastern Grant County?

A. Galatia.

◆

Q. The home of former vice president of the United States Thomas

A. Hendricks was in what Indiana town?

◆

Q. What Clinton County town derived its name from being situated on the Michigan Road?

A. Michigantown.

◆

Q. From what Indiana city did Taylor University relocate to Upland in 1893?

A. Fort Wayne.

◆

Q. What Indiana county was named in honor of a New York governor called the "father of the Erie Canal"?

A. Clinton (for DeWitt Clinton).

◆

Q. What Indiana county seat derives its name from a European city?

A. Frankfort (for Frankfurt am Main, West Germany).

Q. What Carroll County town, founded in 1832, was named for a Wyandotte chief?

A. Burlington.

———◆———

Q. On what road near Kokomo did Elwood Haynes test drive his first mechanically successful automobile on July 4, 1894?

A. Pumpkin Vine Pike.

———◆———

Q. What Indiana town is the home of the unique 1882 two-story cylindrical rotating cellblock jail?

A. Crawfordsville.

———◆———

Q. Where may one tour the restored 1910 Ruthmere Mansion?

A. Elkhart.

———◆———

Q. What is the seat of Union County?

A. Liberty.

———◆———

Q. The historic French Imperial-style Reitz Home is in what Indiana city?

A. Evansville.

———◆———

Q. What town was the western terminus of the Whetzel Trace?

A. Waverly.

Q. The name of a young shepherd in the song, "Pastoral Elegy," from the *Missouri Harmony* songbook provided the basis for naming what Indiana town?

A. Corydon.

———◆———

Q. What Indiana city was previously called Hohman and State Line?

A. Hammond.

———◆———

Q. As an early Quaker settlement, Fountain City was called by what name?

A. Newport.

———◆———

Q. What Pulaski County town was named for a Potawatomi chief who fought in the Battle of Tippecanoe?

A. Winamac.

———◆———

Q. By what name was the community of Howe first called?

A. Lima.

———◆———

Q. In 1843 what community served for a short time as the seat of Noble County?

A. Port Mitchell.

———◆———

Q. What Indiana town is supposedly named for a volcano in Sicily?

A. Mount Etna.

Q. During the gas boom era, what city was known as the "Queen City of the gas belt"?

A. Marion.

Q. What southwest Tippecanoe County community is named for an officer in the War of 1812 and the Black Hawk War?

A. Odell (for Major John W. O'Dell).

Q. What is the seat of Benton County.

A. Fowler.

Q. "Artesian City" is the nickname of what Indiana town?

A. Martinsville.

Q. Harrodsburg was known by what previous name?

A. New Gene.

Q. What two Lawrence County towns are named for the texture and type of limestone found in the area?

A. Oolitic and East Oolitic.

Q. Romona in Owen County was originally called by what name?

A. Brintonville.

Q. During pioneer days, the region around Morocco was known by what name?

A. Beaver Prairie.

Q. What Indiana city has a French name meaning "the door"?

A. LaPorte.

Q. Founded in 1848, what Howard County town is named for a Miami chief?

A. Greentown (for Chief Green).

Q. By what name was New Harmony called by the Rappites?

A. Harmonie.

Q. Rushville and Rush County are named for what signer of the Declaration of Independence?

A. Benjamin F. Rush.

Q. From what Indiana city in 1861 did Ulysses S. Grant telegraph his acceptance of the commission of colonel over the Twenty-First Illinois Regiment.

A. Lafayette.

Q. Fort Wayne is the seat of what county?

A. Allen.

Q. What town on the Mississinewa River in Grant County was platted by Obadiah Jones in 1837?

A. Jonesboro.

———◆———

Q. Saint Joseph's and Southold are both former names of what northern Indiana city?

A. South Bend.

———◆———

Q. What city served as the capital of the Indiana Territory from 1800 to 1813?

A. Vincennes.

———◆———

Q. The Little Pigeon Creek separates what two Indiana counties?

A. Warrick and Spencer.

———◆———

Q. Measuring north to south, what is the longest and narrowest county in Indiana?

A. Vermillion.

———◆———

Q. In what Indiana county will you find Buddha?

A. Lawrence.

———◆———

Q. Due to the gas boom, what Grant County town grew from a small crossroads in 1887 to a population of over 6,000 in four years?

A. Gas City.

Q. "The Snake Hole" was the name of the first saloon in what Grant County community?

A. Upland.

———◆———

Q. Where is the home of Purdue University?

A. West Lafayette.

———◆———

Q. By what name was Odell first called?

A. Odell's Corners.

———◆———

Q. Under what name was Hymera founded in 1870?

A. Pittsburg.

———◆———

Q. Prior to the founding of Sullivan in 1842, what was the seat of Sullivan County?

A. Merom.

———◆———

Q. What Sullivan County town is named for the site in the Bible where Joshua routed the Hazor confederacy?

A. Merom (for Water of Merom).

———◆———

Q. By what name was Oaktown formerly known?

A. Oak Station.

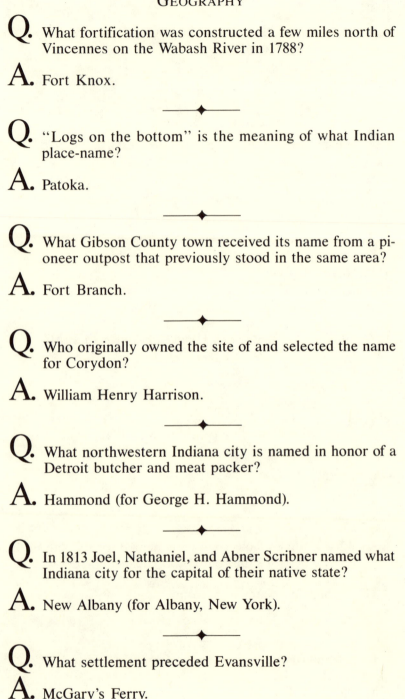

Q. What fortification was constructed a few miles north of Vincennes on the Wabash River in 1788?

A. Fort Knox.

———◆———

Q. "Logs on the bottom" is the meaning of what Indian place-name?

A. Patoka.

———◆———

Q. What Gibson County town received its name from a pioneer outpost that previously stood in the same area?

A. Fort Branch.

———◆———

Q. Who originally owned the site of and selected the name for Corydon?

A. William Henry Harrison.

———◆———

Q. What northwestern Indiana city is named in honor of a Detroit butcher and meat packer?

A. Hammond (for George H. Hammond).

———◆———

Q. In 1813 Joel, Nathaniel, and Abner Scribner named what Indiana city for the capital of their native state?

A. New Albany (for Albany, New York).

———◆———

Q. What settlement preceded Evansville?

A. McGary's Ferry.

ENTERTAINMENT

C H A P T E R   T W O

Q. What noted radio commentator attended Valparaiso University?

A. Lowell Thomas.

Q. Indiana native David Lee Roth was an original member of what rock group in 1974?

A. Van Halen.

Q. In what 1958 science fiction movie did Hoosier Steve McQueen make his screen debut?

A. *The Blob*.

Q. What Brown County attraction opens the world of make-believe with a rousing marionette show?

A. The Melchoir Marionette Theatre.

Q. In 1908 what screen star was born Jane Alice Peters in Fort Wayne?

A. Carole Lombard.

Q. Indiana native Julia Barr potrayed what character in "All My Children"?

A. Brooke English.

———◆———

Q. Jazz great Gary Burton was born in what Indiana city?

A. Anderson.

———◆———

Q. In what television comedy, which first aired in October 1982, did Indiana-born actor Ron Glass star?

A. "The New Odd Couple."

———◆———

Q. Actress Julia Barr played what character in the soap opera "Ryan's Hope"?

A. Renie Szabo.

———◆———

Q. Country music entertainer Red Foley died of a heart attack following an appearance in what Indiana city in 1968?

A. Fort Wayne.

———◆———

Q. What Oscar and Emmy award-winning director was born in Lafayette?

A. John Korty.

———◆———

Q. Born in Macy, what actress made her screen debut in the 1929 movie *Speakeasy*?

A. Lola Lane.

Q. Hoosier actress Shelley Long starred with Henry Winkler in what 1982 movie set in a city morgue?

A. *Night Shift.*

---◆---

Q. In 1957, what Indiana-born actress made her television debut on "General Electric Theater" in "Bitter Choice"

A. Anne Baxter.

---◆---

Q. What longtime Indiana blues figure was fatally shot in Indianapolis in 1962?

A. Francis Hillman ("Scrapper") Blackwell.

---◆---

Q. Indiana native James Best portrayed what character in the television series "The Dukes of Hazzard"?

A. Sheriff Rosco P. Coltrane.

---◆---

Q. What Mishawaka-born brothers have been staff musicians on the NBC "Tonight Show" band?

A. Conte and Pete Candoli.

---◆---

Q. Hoagy Carmichael received an Oscar in 1951 for what show tune?

A. "In the Cool, Cool, Cool of the Evening."

---◆---

Q. What actor was born Ray Canton in South Bend on June 11, 1936?

A. Chad Everett.

Q. What South Bend native founded and became President of Music Corporation of America (MCA) and later served as chairman of the board?

A. Jules Stein.

———◆———

Q. What legendary actor was born in Marion in 1931?

A. James Dean.

———◆———

Q. What famous dancer-choreographer was born in Portland?

A. Twyla Tharp.

———◆———

Q. Betsy Palmer was a regular on the celebrity panel of what long-running game show hosted by Garry Moore?

A. "I've Got A Secret."

———◆———

Q. What Indianapolis-born newscaster replaced Barbara Walters on the "Today Show"?

A. Jane Pauley.

———◆———

Q. Sidney Pollack directed what very successful 1982 movie starring Dustin Hoffman?

A. *Tootsie*.

———◆———

Q. What newsman born in East Chicago joined "ABC World News Tonight" when it was introduced in 1978?

A. Frank Reynolds.

Q. In what county was the 1988 movie *Fresh Horses*, starring Molly Ringwald, partially filmed?

A. Switzerland.

———◆———

Q. On what television series did Indiana-born actor Charles Aidman portray a character named Jeremy?

A. "The Wild Wild West."

———◆———

Q. In what early 1960s domestic sitcom did Indiana-born actor Leon Ames play lawyer Stanley Banks?

A. "Father of the Bride."

———◆———

Q. What 1987-88 movie starring Claude Akins was filmed on location in Greenfield?

A. *Pushed Too Far.*

———◆———

Q. In 1935 what creative blues pianist and singer died at age 30 in Indianapolis from the effects of acute alcoholism?

A. Leroy Carr.

———◆———

Q. What Indiana-born comedian hosted his own television variety show for twenty years?

A. Red Skelton.

———◆———

Q. Where is the Indiana Beach family amusement park situated?

A. Monticello.

Q. What blues musician was born in Indianapolis on January 16, 1928?

A. Edward Lamonte Franklin.

◆

Q. In what year did Hoosier actress Marjorie Main make her screen debut?

A. 1932.

◆

Q. What Indianapolis native became the announcer for "The Burns and Allen Show" in 1951?

A. Harry Von Zell.

◆

Q. In 1982 what was Indiana-born country music singer Janie Fricke's first No. 1 single?

A. "Don't Worry 'Bout Me Baby."

◆

Q. Born in Vincennes, what actress appeared in the 1921 silent film *The Four Horsemen of the Apocalypse*, starring Rudolph Valentino?

A. Alice Terry.

◆

Q. On what label did Indiana blues guitarist Shirley Griffith record?

A. Bluesville.

◆

Q. Where was country music singer Janie Fricke born?

A. South Whitney.

Q. Talk show host David Letterman is a native of what city?

A. Indianapolis.

———◆———

Q. What Indiana-born female county music singer appeared in such movies as *Las Vegas Hillbillies, Road To Nashville,* and *Second Fiddle To A Steel Guitar?*

A. Connie Smith.

———◆———

Q. Indiana native Ken Kercheval became an original cast member of what prime-time television series, playing the role of lawyer Cliff Barnes?

A. "Dallas."

———◆———

Q. What Goodland native was honored by jazz greats at Carnegie Hall in July 1972?

A. Albert Edwin ("Eddie") Condon.

———◆———

Q. Singer-actress Florence Henderson was born in what Indiana community?

A. Dale.

———◆———

Q. The 1938 comedy *Bringing Up Baby,* starring Cary Grant and Katharine Hepburn, was directed by what Hoosier?

A. Howard Hanks.

———◆———

Q. In 1971 what became the first solo hit single by Hoosier singer Michael Jackson?

A. "Got To Be There."

Q. What popular late night talk show host served as a television weatherman in Indianapolis?

A. David Letterman.

—◆—

Q. In what 1944 movie did Indiana native Leon Ames play Judy Garland's sympathetic father?

A. *Meet Me In St. Louis.*

—◆—

Q. What Richmond-born drummer joined the Count Basie group in 1967?

A. Harold J. Jones.

—◆—

Q. In what television sitcom did Indiana native Forrest Tucker play the scheming Sergeant Morgan O'Rourke assigned to Fort Courage?

A. "F Troop."

—◆—

Q. What South Bend native portrayed the level-headed Officer Bobby Hill in the crime show "Hill Street Blues"?

A. Michael Warren.

—◆—

Q. Where was orchestra leader and actor Phil Harris born?

A. Linton.

—◆—

Q. In what 1972 movie did Hoosier James Best appear with Paul Winfield and Cicely Tyson?

A. *Sounder.*

Q. What Indiana-born actor starred as officer Frank Morgan in "Sheriff of Cochise (U.S. Marshal)"?

A. John Bromfield.

———◆———

Q. How many No. 1 hits did the Jackson Five have in 1970?

A. Four.

———◆———

Q. What native Hoosier played the next-door neighbor, Gordon Kirkwood, in the 1960s sitcom "Mister Ed"?

A. Leon Ames.

———◆———

Q. Gene Hackman and Barbara Hershey starred in what classic 1986 basketball movie filmed in rural Indiana?

A. *Hoosiers.*

———◆———

Q. Hoosier Florence Henderson played the mother of her three children and three step-children in what long-running television series.

A. "The Brady Bunch."

———◆———

Q. What internationally known jazz celloist-composer began teaching at Indiana University in 1966?

A. David Nathaniel Baker.

———◆———

Q. What Hoosier native played the first MacKenzie Corey on the television soap opera, "Another World"?

A. Robert Emhardt.

Q. Indiana-born actor Alex Karras played the role of George Papadopolis, an ex-pro football player, in what television sitcom?

A. "Webster."

✦

Q. With what single did LaToya Jackson make her solo debut?

A. "If You Feel The Funk."

✦

Q. What Brazil-born actor-musician had the title rile in the 1938 movie, *Mr. Chump*, with actress Lola Lane?

A. Johnnie ("Scat") Davis.

✦

Q. Singer Connie Smith first reached the top of the country music charts with what recording?

A. "Once A Day."

✦

Q. What 1987 movie, primarily filmed in Indianapolis, starred Charlie Sheen and John Cusack?

A. *Eight Men Out.*

✦

Q. Director-writer-producer Maurice Geraghty, whose television credits include "Bonanza," "The Virginian," and "Daniel Boone," was born in what Indiana community?

A. Rushville.

✦

Q. Where was actor Ron Glass born?

A. Evansville.

Q. What internationally-known gospel music performer and composer was formerly a high school music teacher in Alexandria?

A. Bill Gaither.

━━━━━◆━━━━━

Q. Country music singer Steve Wariner, who grew up in Indiana, had what No. 1 single in 1982?

A. "All Roads Lead To You."

━━━━━◆━━━━━

Q. What 1950 movie starring William Bendix and Allen Martin, Jr. was filmed at the Indiana Boys School?

A. *Johnny Holiday.*

━━━━━◆━━━━━

Q. Country music singer Sylvia was born in what Indiana city?

A. Kokomo.

━━━━━◆━━━━━

Q. Indiana native Carole Lombard married what actor in 1939?

A. Clark Gable.

━━━━━◆━━━━━

Q. Filmed on location in Indianapolis, what 1969 movie starred Paul Newman and Joanne Woodward?

A. *Winning.*

━━━━━◆━━━━━

Q. What Columbus-born singer was spokesman for the successful singing group, The Four Freshmen?

A. Ross Edwin Barbour.

Q. Musician Gary Burton has been the recipient of how many Grammys?

A. Three.

———◆———

Q. In what 1935 movie did Hoosier actor Charles Butterworth portray Willis, a shy clerk mistaken for Public Enemy No. 2?

A. *Baby Face Harrington.*

———◆———

Q. What Hoosier native created a lasting impression as Bette Davis's greedy brother, Oscar Hubbard, in the 1941 film *The Little Foxes.*

A. Charles Dingle.

———◆———

Q. Indiana native Chad Everett made his television debut in what 1960s detective series?

A. "Hawaiian Eye."

———◆———

Q. Indiana native Anne Baxter received an Oscar for best supporting actress in what 1946 movie?

A. *The Razor's Edge.*

———◆———

Q. Directing and producing *The Sound of Music* in 1965 garnered what Indiana native two Oscars?

A. Robert Wise.

———◆———

Q. Indiana-born Jo Anne Worley was a regular on what fast-paced television comedy show beginning in 1968?

A. "Laugh-In."

Q. Indiana native Dick York portrayed what character on the television sitcom "Bewitched" from 1964 to 1969?

A. Darin Stevens.

◆

Q. What actor played George Gipp in the 1940 film *Knute Rockne—All American*?

A. Ronald Reagan.

◆

Q. What 1989 Academy Award-winning movie, partially filmed in Franklin County, starred Dustin Hoffman and Tom Cruise?

A. *Rain Man.*

◆

Q. Dectective Ron Harris in the television series "Barney Miller" was played by what Indiana-born actor?

A. Ron Glass.

◆

Q. Country and western singer Connie Smith was born in what Indiana city on August 14, 1941?

A. Elkhart.

◆

Q. Hoosier native Phil Harris appeared in what 1957 movie starring John Wayne?

A. *The High and the Mighty.*

◆

Q. Hoosier Ken Kercheval played the part of Nick Hunter on what long-running daytime soap opera?

A. "Search for Tomorrow."

Q. Comedian Red Skelton was born in what Indiana city?

A. Vincennes.

———◆———

Q. In what 1989 movie does Shelley Long play the role of a spoiled housewife and compulsive shopper who takes a group of rich Beverly Hills girls on a scouting trip?

A. *Troop Beverly Hills.*

———◆———

Q. In what city was actor Forrest Tucker born?

A. Plainfield.

———◆———

Q. Indiana native James Louis ("J. J.") Johnson is known for his expertise on what instrument?

A. Trombone.

———◆———

Q. What film began the "Ma and Pa Kettle" series for Indiana-born actress Marjorie Main?

A. *The Egg and I.*

———◆———

Q. Television sportscaster Chris Schenkel was born in what Indiana community.

A. Bippus.

———◆———

Q. What Indianapolis-born jazz musician won a Grammy award in 1972 for his album "First Light"?

A. Frederick ("Freddie") Hubbard.

Q. What Indiana-born character actor portrayed the butler, Groves, who becomes interested in Mae West in the 1937 movie, *Every Day's a Holiday?*

A. Charles Butterworth.

———◆———

Q. Indiana-born actor James Dean selected what 1955 movie for his first starring role?

A. *East of Eden.*

———◆———

Q. What 1982 Michael Jackson album became the most successful LP in record history?

A. "Thriller."

———◆———

Q. Where is the Cedar Valley Spring Bluegrass Festival held?

A. Derby.

———◆———

Q. What 1981 movie, filmed primarily in East Chicago, told the story of a young Yugoslavian boy and his peers in the 1960s?

A. *Four Friends.*

———◆———

Q. The Academy of Country Music voted what Indiana native Female Vocalist of the Year in 1984?

A. Janie Fricke.

———◆———

Q. The movie *Out of Africa* was directed by what Hoosier?

A. Sydney Pollack.

Q. Joseph Jackson, father of the Jackson Five, played guitar with what local group while working at Inland Steel Company in Gary?

A. The Falcons.

Q. Where was singer-songwriter John Cougar Mellencamp born on October 7, 1951?

A. Seymour.

Q. Plainfield offered the location for the filming of what 1950 motion picture?

A. *Johnny Holiday*.

Q. John Carradine starred in what 1984 "After School TV Special" filmed primarily in French Lick?

A. "Umbrella Jack".

Q. Actor Dick York was born in what Indiana city?

A. Fort Wayne.

Q. Where was the world premiere of the movie *Knute Rockne—All American* held on October 4, 1940?

A. South Bend.

Q. In what Indiana community was actress Jo Anne Worley born?

A. Lowell.

Q. Partially filmed in Bloomington, what 1979 movie climaxes in a bike race?

A. *Breaking Away.*

———◆———

Q. The Indiana Friends of Bluegrass Festival is held each spring and fall in what Indiana town?

A. Noblesville.

———◆———

Q. In what sitcom did Shelley Long play the part of barmaid Diane Chambers?

A. "Cheers."

———◆———

Q. Indianapolis and Bloomington hosted the filming of what 1987 movie starring Linda Purl?

A. *Viper.*

———◆———

Q. Renowned producer-director Robert Wise was born in what Indiana town?

A. Winchester.

———◆———

Q. Actress Lee Remick starred in what 1975 movie filmed primarily in and around Vevay?

A. *A Girl Named Sooner.*

———◆———

Q. In what Indiana city was actress and television personality Betsy Palmer born?

A. East Chicago.

Q. Who starred in the 1937 movie *Hoosier Schoolboy*?

A. Mickey Rooney.

Q. What is Red Skelton's given name?

A. Richard.

Q. Indiana-born actor Robert Emhardt played syndicate director Earl Connors in what 1961 movie?

A. *Underworld U.S.A.*

Q. What vaudeville ventriloquist turned cowboy actor was born in Franklin on February 12, 1891?

A. Max Terhune.

Q. What Indianapolis-born musician wrote the scores for such movies as, *Top of the Heap*, *Cleopatra Jones*, and *Willie Dynamite*?

A. James Louis ("J. J.") Johnson.

Q. By what nickname was Indiana-born blues musician Edward Lamonte Franklin known?

A. "Guitar Pete."

Q. On what date did Indiana-born country music singer Connie Smith become a member of the Grand Ole Opry?

A. June 13, 1965.

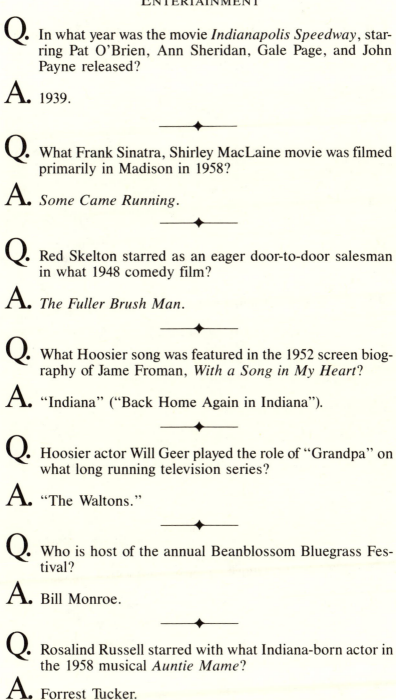

Q. In what year was the movie *Indianapolis Speedway*, starring Pat O'Brien, Ann Sheridan, Gale Page, and John Payne released?

A. 1939.

◆

Q. What Frank Sinatra, Shirley MacLaine movie was filmed primarily in Madison in 1958?

A. *Some Came Running.*

◆

Q. Red Skelton starred as an eager door-to-door salesman in what 1948 comedy film?

A. *The Fuller Brush Man.*

◆

Q. What Hoosier song was featured in the 1952 screen biography of Jame Froman, *With a Song in My Heart*?

A. "Indiana" ("Back Home Again in Indiana").

◆

Q. Hoosier actor Will Geer played the role of "Grandpa" on what long running television series?

A. "The Waltons."

◆

Q. Who is host of the annual Beanblossom Bluegrass Festival?

A. Bill Monroe.

◆

Q. Rosalind Russell starred with what Indiana-born actor in the 1958 musical *Auntie Mame*?

A. Forrest Tucker.

Q. While working with Gene Autry, Hoosier-born performer and actor Max Terhune joined what popular country-western radio program in 1933?

A. "National Barn Dance."

◆

Q. Where were the brothers who made up the Jackson Five born?

A. Gary.

◆

Q. What Indiana-born singer recorded such albums as "Night Dancin'" (1980) and "American Fool" (1982)?

A. John Cougar Mellencamp.

◆

Q. What 1942 film was the last movie made by Hoosier actress Carole Lombard?

A. *To Be or Not to Be.*

◆

Q. What was Steve McQueen's actual full name?

A. Terence Steven McQueen.

◆

Q. Michael Warren, born in Indiana, portrayed P. J. Lewis in what NBC hour-long adventure series?

A. "Sierra."

◆

Q. What actor was born in Wabash on December 28, 1887?

A. Charles Dingle.

Q. Indiana native Robert Wise received two Oscars in 1961 for directing and producing what movie?

A. *West Side Story.*

———◆———

Q. What Gary-born actor portrayed Steve Bruce, boyfriend of Diahann Carroll, in the television series "Julia"?

A. Fred Williamson.

———◆———

Q. Director Sydney Pollack is a native of what Indiana city?

A. South Bend.

———◆———

Q. What 1943 movie featuring George D. Hay, Dale Evans, George Byron, and Thurston Hall, revolved around a country novelty band called the "Hoosier Hotshots"?

A. *Hoosier Holiday.*

———◆———

Q. What 1935 movie starring Norman Foster features an ex-Union soldier turned school teacher, dealing with government corruption in a small Indiana town?

A. *Hoosier Schoolmaster.*

———◆———

Q. Where was actor Charles Butterworth born in 1896?

A. South Bend.

———◆———

Q. Actor-writer-director Charles Aidman was born in what Indiana town in 1929?

A. Frankfort.

Q. Where was actress Shelley Long born?

A. Fort Wayne.

◆

Q. The Isham Jones orchestra introduced and popularized what 1923 song?

A. "Indiana Moon."

◆

Q. What bluegrass celebration is held each August in Lake County?

A. Stoney River Bluegrass Festival.

◆

Q. What Indiana-born actress starred in the 1980 thriller, *Friday the 13th*?

A. Betsy Palmer.

◆

Q. In what Indiana city was actor Robert Emhardt born on July 16, 1916?

A. Indianapolis.

◆

Q. What Indiana-born actor participated in 24 of *The Range Busters* episodes with fellow actors Ray Corrigan and John King?

A. Max Terhune.

◆

Q. What 1968 movie starring Steve McQueen and Jacqueline Bisset became famous for its innovative car chase scene?

A. *Bullitt*.

Q. In what Indiana community was actress Marjorie Main born?

A. Acton.

———◆———

Q. In what 1956 movie did Hoosier actor James Dean co-star with Rock Hudson and Elizabeth Taylor?

A. *Giant*.

———◆———

Q. Actor Ken Kercheval was born in what northeastern Indiana community?

A. Wolcottville.

———◆———

Q. In 1983 what two singles went to No. 1 for Indiana native Michael Jackson?

A. "Billie Jean" and "Beat It."

———◆———

Q. What Indiana college did entertainer David Letterman attend?

A. Ball State University.

———◆———

Q. Hoosier actress Anne Baxter appeared in what 1956 biblical epic?

A. *The Ten Commandments*.

———◆———

Q. What Hoosier humorist first appeared on television in 1949 with a thrice-weekly, five-minute program on CBS?

A. Herb Shriner.

Q. Indiana native Michael Jackson starred with Diana Ross in what 1978 motion picture?

A. *The Wiz.*

◆

Q. What Indiana-born actor made his screen debut in the 1940 movie, *The Westerner?*

A. Forrest Tucker.

◆

Q. What Hoosier portrayed strong man Willy Armitage in the television adventure series "Mission Impossible?"

A. Peter Lupus.

◆

Q. Where was rock music star David Lee Roth born?

A. Bloomington.

◆

Q. Hoosier Karl Malden portrayed detective lieutenant Mike Stone in what 1970s television show?

A. "The Streets of San Francisco."

◆

Q. Indiana native Charles Dingle portrayed Andrew Holmes, a factory worker who stirred up trouble for Cary Grant, in what 1942 movie?

A. *The Talk of the Town.*

◆

Q. What prolific Indiana writer of children's literature created the *Little Colonel* series?

A. Annie Fellows Johnston.

HISTORY

Q. During what years were Marmon automobiles built in Indianapolis?

A. From 1902 through 1933.

———◆———

Q. What famous nineteenth-century Presbyterian minister held his first pastorate in Lawrenceburg from 1837 to 1839?

A. Henry Ward Beecher.

———◆———

Q. In 1865 legislation was passed in Indiana allowing blacks what judicial right?

A. To testify in court.

———◆———

Q. How many accused robbers were lynched by a vigilante mob of 400 at Versailles in 1897?

A. Five.

———◆———

Q. Whose body laid in state in the capitol building at Indianapolis on April 30, 1865?

A. Abraham Lincoln.

Q. On what date was the State of Indiana admitted into the Union?

A. December 11, 1816.

Q. In 1870, what railroad company established its shops in Elkhart?

A. Michigan Southern Railway Company.

Q. What were the casualty figures of government troops from the 1811 Battle of Tippecanoe?

A. 61 killed, 127 seriously wounded.

Q. On February 10, 1925, the General Assembly assigned what official designation to the date of December 11?

A. Indiana Day.

Q. What was Johnny Appleseed's actual name?

A. John Chapman.

Q. What Knox County resident served as the first Speaker of the House of the Indiana General Assembly?

A. Isaac Blackford.

Q. In 1838 what Indian tribe was escorted out of Indiana by the military?

A. Potawatomi.

Q. What Indiana politician made the famous remark, "What this country really needs is a good five-cent cigar"?

A. Thomas Riley Marshall.

Q. In 1859 who became the first woman to address the Indiana Legislature?

A. Dr. Mary F. Thomas.

Q. What was the per acre cash value of improved land in Indiana in 1850?

A. Eleven dollars.

Q. During the early 1880s, what became the leading labor organization in Indiana?

A. The Knights of Labor.

Q. What champion of public schools in Indiana made his first plea before the legislature in 1846?

A. Caleb Mills.

Q. Who in 1967 became the first black to be elected mayor of Gary?

A. Richard G. Hatcher.

Q. What pioneer route connected New Albany with Vincennes?

A. Buffalo Trace.

Q. In 1819 who became the first couple married in a Christian wedding ceremony in Parke County?

A. Mary Ann Isaacs and Cheif Christmas Dazney.

———◆———

Q. Who served as governor of Indiana during the Civil War years?

A. Oliver P. Morton.

———◆———

Q. George W. Julian was the vice-presidential nominee for what party in 1852?

A. Free Soil.

———◆———

Q. Who platted Elkhart in 1832?

A. Dr. Havilah Beardsley.

———◆———

Q. In 1850 approximately what percentage of Indiana's population was rural?

A. Ninety-five percent.

———◆———

Q. From what university did Dan Quayle receive a law degree in 1974?

A. Indiana University School of Law.

———◆———

Q. What two Auburn brothers who owned a local carriage maunfacturing firm established the Auburn Automobile Company in 1900?

A. Frank and Morris Eckhart.

Q. What was the total value of farm implements in Indiana in 1860?

A. Nearly $10,500,000.

Q. In 1852, who became Indiana's first state superintendent of public school?

A. William C. Larrabee.

Q. What religious denomination founded Huntington College in 1897 after their Hartsville buildings burned?

A. Church of the United Brethern in Christ.

Q. How old was La Fontaine when he became chief of the Miami Indians in 1828?

A. Eighteen.

Q. What noted educator of the the early twentieth century was born in Andrews?

A. Ellwood Patterson Cubberley.

Q. The census of 1800 showed how many persons living in Indiana Territory?

A. 5,641.

Q. By 1820, how many county governments existed in Indiana?

A. Thirty-five.

Q. In what facility was the inaugural ball of the first governor of the state of Indiana held?

A. Green Tree Tavern (Charlestown).

Q. What was the average cost of the 666 new public schoolhouses that were constructed in Indiana during 1859?

A. $439.67.

Q. In 1838 what financial disaster befell the state government of Indiana?

A. Bankruptcy.

Q. Who was the featured guest speaker at the Michigan City Fourth of July celebration in 1837?

A. Daniel Webster.

Q. What firm built their first electric buggy in New Chicago in 1898?

A. United States Electric Carriage Company.

Q. In 1854, what was the average length of the annual school term in Indiana?

A. Just over two and one-half months.

Q. What speed limit was established by the 1925 Indiana General Assembly for state highways?

A. 35 miles per hour.

Q. In 1815 how many regularly licensed ferries were operating in Clark County?

A. Ten.

———◆———

Q. Who founded the Roanoke Classical Seminary in 1861?

A. Frederick S. Reefy.

———◆———

Q. What resident of Knightstown was a former captain in Napoleon's army?

A. Count Lehmanowsky.

———◆———

Q. In whose Dublin home did the first woman's suffrage group in Indiana meet in 1851?

A. Amanda Way.

———◆———

Q. What was the average monthly pay for women public school teachers in Indiana in 1853?

A. Less than ten dollars.

———◆———

Q. Where was the miniature Crosley automobile first offered for sale on April 28, 1939?

A. Richmond.

———◆———

Q. Who was sent by George Rogers Clark in July 1778 to secure the allegiance of the residents of Vincennes to the United States?

A. Father Pierre Gilbault.

Q. Made up of Indiana National Guardsmen, what was the only distinctly Indiana outfit to serve in World War I?

A. 115th Field Artillery.

———◆———

Q. In 1852 what two Indiana cities instituted free schools based on a graded system?

A. Madison and Richmond.

———◆———

Q. During whose administration did Indiana's Thomas Riley Marshall serve two terms as vice president of the United States?

A. Woodrow Wilson.

———◆———

Q. What famous evangelist developed a religious center at Winona Lake in the first third of the twentieth century?

A. Billy Sunday.

———◆———

Q. What major railroad passenger facility, the first of its kind in the nation, was opened in Indianapolis on September 20, 1853?

A. Union Station.

———◆———

Q. During the heyday of the Wabash and Erie Canal, what Fort Wayne establishment was the most popular amusement palace along the canal?

A. Vermilyea Tavern.

Q. Having lived to the age of 105 years, what granddaughter of Miami Indian chief Little Turtle is buried at Roanoke?

A. Kilsoquah.

Q. In 1850 how many miles of railroad tracks were in actual operation in Indiana?

A. 212.

Q. By 1880, how much money was invested in manufacturing in Indiana?

A. Over $65,000,000.

Q. What Anderson firm was acquired by General Motors in 1919?

A. Remy Electric Company.

Q. During the 1850s, what became the most widely used gauge of railroad track in Indiana?

A. 4 feet, 8 inches.

Q. Who in 1828 became the first permanent settler of Logansport?

A. Alexander Chamberlain.

Q. What school established in 1917 by the Church of God evolved into Anderson College?

A. Anderson Bible Training School.

HISTORY

Q. What correctional facility was opened near Putnamville in 1915?

A. Indiana State Farm (now Putnamville State Farm).

Q. The Indian Treaty of 1809 created the boundary of what white settlement?

A. Ten O'Clock Line.

Q. What Crawfordsville resident served as the territorial governor of New Mexico from 1878 to 1881?

A. Lew Wallace.

Q. In 1903 what United States Army facility was established in Marion County?

A. Fort Benjamin Harrison.

Q. In 1884 what religious sect established Manchester College in North Manchester?

A. Dunkers.

Q. Under what name was Valparaiso University established as a Methodist school in 1859?

A. Valparaiso Male and Female College.

Q. What Indiana congressman introduced the first resolution for a woman-suffrage amendment in 1868?

A. George W. Julian.

Q. The selection of a rooster for the emblem of the Democratic party during the elections of 1840 evolved from the oratory "crowing" of what Greenfield politician and tavern owner?

A. Joseph Chapman.

Q. Under what name was DePauw University originally founded by the Methodist Episcopal Church in 1837?

A. Indiana Asbury University.

Q. What manufacturer of railroad freight and passenger cars was established in Clarksville on June 1, 1864?

A. Ohio Falls Car and Locomotive Company.

Q. In what year did the Indiana General Assembly pass the first comprehensive Pure Food and Drug Act?

A. 1889.

Q. Who served as the first headmaster of Jefferson Academy, from which today's Vincennes University evolved?

A. Father James Francis Rivet.

Q. Where in Indiana was the 1870 Woolen Exposition held?

A. Indianapolis.

Q. Who was Lake County's first justice of the peace?

A. Solon Robinson.

Q. In 1834 what institution, along with its branches, began serving the banking needs of Indiana?

A. Second State Bank.

———◆———

Q. On what date was sterilization legislation passed in Indiana?

A. March 9, 1907.

———◆———

Q. In whose home in Madison was the Grand Masonic Lodge of Indiana organized in 1818?

A. Major Alexander Chalmers Lanier.

———◆———

Q. On July 1, 1929, what type of retail business came under a special tax in Indiana?

A. Chain stores.

———◆———

Q. What Pulitzer Prize-winning news correspondent during World War II was born near Dana in 1900?

A. Ernie Pyle.

———◆———

Q. In 1816 who became the first state representative from Warrick County?

A. Ratliff Boon.

———◆———

Q. Who defeated Benjamin Harrison in 1876 to become Indiana's seventeenth governor?

A. James D. ("Blue Jeans") Williams.

Q. Lew Wallace's gallantry at Fort Donelson during the Civil War earned him what commission?

A. Major general.

———◆———

Q. What was the only year Studebaker offered the Power Hawk model automobile?

A. 1956.

———◆———

Q. In what year did Indianapolis resident Robert L. Brokenburr become the first black Indiana state senator?

A. 1940.

———◆———

Q. What trade union attempted in 1863 to force the owners of the Indianapolis *Sentinel* to increase wages by twenty percent?

A. Typographical Union.

———◆———

Q. Who was the first governor of Indiana?

A. Jonathan Jennings.

———◆———

Q. What labor organization was established in Indianapolis in 1876?

A. Brotherhood of Locomotive Firemen.

———◆———

Q. In 1841 where was the first thresher manufactured in Indiana?

A. Richmond.

Q. What piece of legislation passed by the General Assembly in 1935 called for the organization of cooperatives for distribution of electricity to rural areas?

A. The Indiana REMC Act.

———◆———

Q. In what Indiana city did the Ancient Order of United Workmen establish a branch in 1873?

A. Terre Haute.

———◆———

Q. In 1905 the Indiana General Assembly passed a law carrying fines up to five hundred dollars and jail terms up to six months for the sale, manufacture, or possession of what consumer item?

A. Cigarettes.

———◆———

Q. Where in Indiana was self-liquidating scrip money issued on March 8, 1933?

A. Franklin.

———◆———

Q. Women were first admitted to the University of Notre Dame in what year?

A. 1972.

———◆———

Q. What official slogan or motto for Indiana was adopted by the General Assembly in 1937?

A. "The Crossroads of America."

Q. During World War II, where did E. I. du Pont de Nemours and Company construct the world's largest gunpowder plant?

A. Charlestown.

---◆---

Q. What was the first institution of higher learning to be established in Orange County?

A. Lick Creek Friends College.

---◆---

Q. In 1853 what became the first major public building to be constructed of Indiana limestone?

A. United States Customs and Courthouse, Louisville, Kentucky.

---◆---

Q. For how many years was Abraham Lincoln a resident of Indiana?

A. Fourteen.

---◆---

Q. What nineteenth-century Potawatomi Indian leader attended both Notre Dame University and Oberlin College?

A. Chief Simon Pokagon.

---◆---

Q. What Cord automobile introduced in 1935 was designed by Gordon Buehrig and was known for its retractable headlights and distinctive "coffin-nosed" front end?

A. Model 810.

Q. What structure served as the first meeting place of the Indiana General Assembly?

A. Harrison County Courthouse.

———◆———

Q. Who laid out Crawfordsville in 1823?

A. Major Ambrose Whitlock.

———◆———

Q. Making her legislative debut during the 1921 session, who was the first woman to be elected an Indiana state representative?

A. Julia D. Nelson.

———◆———

Q. The Duesenberg Motor Company of Indianapolis offered its first production car in what year?

A. 1920.

———◆———

Q. In 1859 what percentage of public school teachers in Indiana were women?

A. Twenty percent.

———◆———

Q. In the 1860 elections, what Crawfordsville resident was elected governor of Indiana?

A. Henry Smith Lane.

———◆———

Q. What fiery Covington politician was appointed minister to Prussia in 1849?

A. Edward A. Hannegan.

Q. Employing between 300 and 400 persons, what was the largest single manufacturing establishment in Indiana in 1850?

A. Indiana Cotton Mills in Cannelton.

Q. Who aquired the New Albany Glass Works in 1872?

A. W. C. DePauw.

Q. In 1860 where did Indianapolis rank in population, compared to other U.S. cities?

A. Forty-eight.

Q. As a leader in the Northwest Boundary dispute, Indiana senator Edward A. Hannegan coined what slogan?

A. "Fifty-Four Forty or Fight."

Q. By 1876, how many schoolhouses existed in Indiana?

A. 9,434.

Q. At the close of the French and Indian War in 1763, what nation gained title to the Mississippi Valley and the Louisiana region?

A. England.

Q. During the 1830s, what was the price of split rails for fencing material?

A. One cent per rail.

Q. Indiana's oldest farm organization, the Order of Patrons of Husbandry, which came to the state in 1869, used what term to designate local units?

A. "Grange."

———◆———

Q. In what county was the American Cannel Coal Company organized by eastern capitalists in the 1840s?

A. Perry.

———◆———

Q. What Madison resident advanced Indiana approximately $1,000,000 in the form of an unsecured loan to enable the equipping of soldiers during the Civil War?

A. James F. D. Lanier.

———◆———

Q. What percentage of the total student body in Indiana in 1879 attend rural township schools?

A. Seventy-two percent.

———◆———

Q. Aside from a few early missionary ventures by French Jesuits, who became the first European to explore the Indiana area in 1679?

A. Robert Cavelier, Sieur de la Salle.

———◆———

Q. Founded in Jefferson County in 1827, what is the oldest private institution of higher learning in Indiana?

A. Hanover College.

Q. What labor organization met in Indianapolis in June 1850 to draw up a constitution and statement of objectives?

A. Mechanics Mutual Protections.

———◆———

Q. How many Studebaker automobiles were sold in 1915?

A. Over 45,000.

———◆———

Q. What institution in 1863 became the First National Bank of Evansville?

A. Canal Bank.

———◆———

Q. During the 1880s, what was the leading nationality of foreign-born workers employed in manufacturing and mining jobs in Indiana?

A. Germans.

———◆———

Q. What famous steamboat was built at New Albany in 1866 for Captain John W. Cannon?

A. The *Robert E. Lee*.

———◆———

Q. By 1861, how many free banks were operating in Indiana?

A. Seventeen.

———◆———

Q. What was the average annual income for industrial workers in Indianapolis in 1880?

A. 391 dollars.

Q. What was the value of walnut logs shipped to Europe from Whitley County in 1875?

A. Over fifty thousand dollars.

———◆———

Q. What Jackson County outlaws committed what has been called "the world's first train robbery" at Seymour on the evening of October 6, 1866?

A. Reno gang.

———◆———

Q. To what location did the legislature move the Indiana State Prison in 1842, with new facilities completed in 1845?

A. Clarksville.

———◆———

Q. Who was known as the "Patriot Priest of the Old Northwest"?

A. Father Pierre Gibault.

———◆———

Q. In 1879 stone from Indiana was first shipped to New York to be used in the construction of whose home?

A. William K. Vanderbilt.

———◆———

Q. In an attempt to encourage the investment of capital for manufacturing purposes, the legislature in 1850 made it possible for what number of persons to incorporate in Indiana?

A. Seven or more.

Q. The Wabash and Erie Canal was completed to Evansville in what year?

A. 1853.

———◆———

Q. What planned community was established in Adams County in 1935, under the direction of the Resettlement Administration, to provide homes for displaced families and part-time workers?

A. Decatur Homesteads.

———◆———

Q. Approximately how many fugitive slaves were sheltered at Levi Coffin's home in Fountain City between 1827 and 1847?

A. Two thousand.

———◆———

Q. The Mennonite Book Concern, which evolved out of a small bookstore and print shop, was established in what Indiana town in 1893?

A. Berne.

———◆———

Q. How many workers on the Wabash and Erie Canal died of cholera in 1850?

A. 150.

———◆———

Q. The Indiana legislature extended what right to married women with regard to estates in 1846?

A. Right to make wills.

Q. Who piloted the balloon that lifted off from Lafayette on August 17, 1859, carrying the nation's first mail by air?

A. John Wise.

———◆———

Q. The Oliver Plow Works of South Bend broke into the international marketplace in 1879 by arranging for the distribution of their products in what country?

A. Great Britain.

———◆———

Q. In what year did Henry and Clem Studebaker open a blacksmith and wagon shop in South Bend?

A. 1852.

———◆———

Q. How many Hoosiers served in the military during World War I?

A. 130,670.

———◆———

Q. On August 24, 1805, what firm, with Aaron Burr as a member of the board of directors, was chartered by the Indiana Territorial Legislature to build a canal around the Ohio Falls?

A. The Indiana Canal Company.

———◆———

Q. In 1719–20, what was the second major French fortification to be built in Indiana country?

A. Fort Ouiatenon.

HISTORY

Q. By what name were the United Society of Believers in Christ's Second Appearance known, who established a community in northern Knox County in 1804?

A. Shakers.

───────◆───────

Q. How old was Abraham Lincoln when his mother Nancy Hanks Lincoln died in Spencer County on October 5, 1818?

A. Nine years old.

───────◆───────

Q. What is the nation's oldest Catholic liberal arts college for women?

A. Saint Mary-of-the-Woods College.

───────◆───────

Q. In 1847 where was the first submarine launched in Great Lakes waters?

A. Michigan City.

───────◆───────

Q. Featuring homes dating from 1849, what is the name of Terre Haute's historic district?

A. Farrington's Grove.

───────◆───────

Q. What act by the British in 1774 was designed to stabilize government in the northwest by placing the region under the jurisdiction of the Province of Quebec?

A. The Quebec Act.

Q. In 1850 what city led the state as a center of trade and industry?

A. Madison.

---◆---

Q. By 1856, how many public schools existed in Indianapolis?

A. Twenty.

---◆---

Q. In an attempt to control marketing, what organization was founded in Indianapolis in 1902, to compel profitable prices for all agricultural products?

A. The American Society of Equity.

---◆---

Q. The legendary "white Indians" who supposedly inhabited the site of present-day Clarksville, are said to have been descendents of twelfth-century Welshmen who came to North America under whose leadership?

A. Prince Madoc.

---◆---

Q. Ohio valley industrialist Thomas Gaff built what Italian Renaissance-style villa in Aurora around 1856?

A. Hillforest.

---◆---

Q. Taking seven years and thirty-six lives to construct, in what year was the Big Four Bridge opened across the Ohio River at Jeffersonville?

A. 1895.

Q. Who led troops against Indian forces at the Battle of Tippecanoe on November 7, 1811?

A. General William Henry Harrison.

———◆———

Q. Elected to the 1943 session, who became the first woman to become a part of the Indiana Senate?

A. Arcada Balz.

———◆———

Q. When was the present-day Indiana Farmers Union chartered?

A. September 1954.

———◆———

Q. In February 1933, what Indiana governor was granted almost dictatorial power through a drastic reorganization of the State governmental structure?

A. Paul V. McNutt.

———◆———

Q. In 1880 how many sawmills were in operation in Indiana?

A. Over 2,022.

———◆———

Q. What old military road ran between Fort Wayne and Decatur?

A. Wayne Trace.

———◆———

Q. In 1880 what Marion County resident became the first black member of the Indiana House of Representatives?

A. James S. Hinton.

Q. What was Wendell L. Willkie's actual first name which, due to an Army clerical error, was switched with his middle name during the first World War?

A. Lewis.

———◆———

Q. In what year was the Wabash and Erie Canal finally abandoned to fall into complete disuse?

A. 1874.

———◆———

Q. During the 1850–51 session of the legislature how many plank-road companies were chartered to operate in Indiana?

A. Over thirty.

———◆———

Q. Who was owner of the first railroad in Indiana?

A. Judge W. J. Peasley.

———◆———

Q. The supercharged boat-tailed Auburn sports cars introduced in 1935 were guaranteed by the company to have been individually test driven at what speed before being shipped from the factory?

A. One hundred miles per hour.

———◆———

Q. Under pressure from the public schools, Indiana University removed what subject from its admission requirements in 1873?

A. Greek.

Q. The over 4,000 Indiana manufacturing firms listed in the 1850 United States census employed how many persons?

A. Just over 14,000.

---◆---

Q. During the 1850s, approximately how many vessels were constructed at Madison?

A. 375.

---◆---

Q. Where in 1878 were Studebaker wagons displayed to the international market?

A. Paris Exposition.

---◆---

Q. In what year was the first female student admitted to Indiana University?

A. 1867.

---◆---

Q. In 1873 the nation's first belt railroad was built around what Indiana city?

A. Indianapolis.

---◆---

Q. In 1875 where did Indianapolis rank among other U.S. cities as a pork-packing center?

A. Forth.

---◆---

Q. What two factions among Presbyterians created problems for Wabash College in its early days?

A. "Old Light" and "New Light" Presbyterians.

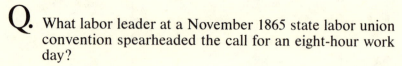

Q. What labor leader at a November 1865 state labor union convention spearheaded the call for an eight-hour work day?

A. John Fehrenbatch.

◆

Q. In what year was the first state primary election held in Indiana?

A. 1916.

◆

Q. What was the population of Indiana in 1920?

A. 2,930,390.

◆

Q. During the Civil War, what portion of Henry County's male population served under the command of Major General William Grose?

A. Approximately fifteen percent.

◆

Q. In what year did the legislature vote to establish public but separate schools for blacks in Indiana?

A. 1869.

◆

Q. What was the population of Indiana in 1920?

A. 2,930,390.

◆

Q. How long did the first session of the Indiana General Assembly last?

A. Sixty-one days.

Q. What labor leader at a November 1865 state labor union convention spearheaded the call for an eight-hour work day?

A. John Fehrenbatch.

Q. In what year was the first state primary election held in Indiana?

A. 1916.

Q. During the Civil War, what portion of Henry County's male population served under the command of Major General William Grose?

A. Approximately fifteen percent.

Q. In what year did the legislature vote to establish public but separate schools for blacks in Indiana?

A. 1869.

Q. Where was the most serious rioting in Indiana during the December 1873 strike of the Brotherhood of Locomotive Engineers against the Pennsylvania Railroad Company?

A. Logansport.

Q. According to census figures, what was the rate of illiteracy in Indiana in 1870?

A. Seven and one-half percent.

Q. The Eleutherian Institute, which became a center of antislavery activities, was founded in Jefferson County by what Baptist minister?

A. Reverend Thomas Craven.

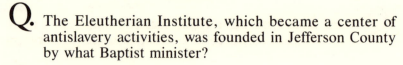

Q. Where in Indiana did the Singer Sewing Machine Company open a branch factory in 1868?

A. South Bend.

Q. Fort Wayne College was formed in 1855 by merging what two institutions?

A. Fort Wayne Female College and Fort Wayne Collegiate Institute.

Q. The Howard brothers of Jeffersonville built what 300-foot vessel in 1853 to carry mail between Louisville and Cincinnati?

A. The *Ben Franklin.*

Q. Where did the Sisters of St. Francis establish a village school in 1851?

A. Oldenburg.

Q. Sylvan Lake was built in 1837 to serve as a feeder for what proposed canal?

A. Michigan and Erie Canal.

Q. What short-lived educational institution was opened by member of the Universalist Church at Logansport in 1872?

A. Smithson College.

Q. To what Indianapolis office was Benjamin Harrison elected in 1857?

A. City Attorney.

Q. What Terre Haute resident founded the nation's first industrial labor union, the American Railway Union?

A. Eugene V. Debs.

Q. By what name were the gangs of horse thieves and counterfeiters who hid in the then dense tamarack swamps of Noble County called during the 1830s and 40s?

A. "Blacklegs."

Q. What 1894 institution of higher learning became Goshen College in 1903?

A. Elkhart Academy.

Q. Although Troy, New York, claims to be the final resting place of *the* Samuel Wilson around whom, according to tradition, the character of "Uncle Sam" evolved, what Indiana community lays the same claim to a Samuel Wilson buried in their local cemetery?

A. Merriam.

Q. What meat-packing company with international interests began operation in Indianapolis in 1864?

A. Kingan and Company.

◆

Q. Who conducted the Wolcottville Seminary from 1852 to 1868?

A. Miss Susan Griggs.

◆

Q. Misunderstandings by local surveyors when the Michigan and Indiana state line was being established originally placed the line how much south of its present-day location?

A. Ten miles.

◆

Q. Where on January 25, 1952, was the nation's first fully automatic railroad freight yard put into operation?

A. Gary.

◆

Q. In what year was the Studebaker Corporation formed?

A. 1868.

◆

Q. How many blacks were residents of Indiana in 1850?

A. 11,262.

◆

Q. What sewing machine manufacturer established a branch factory in Peru in 1870?

A. Howe Sewing Maching Company.

Q. In what year did Indiana pass the State Workmen's Compensation Act?

A. 1914.

———————◆———————

Q. The Henry County Historical Society is housed in what Civil War Major General's home?

A. William Grose.

———————◆———————

Q. At what price did Duesenberg Motor Company offer chassis to custom coach builders in 1929?

A. 8,500 dollars.

———————◆———————

Q. What college was moved from Fort Wayne to Upland in 1893?

A. Taylor University.

———————◆———————

Q. Employing some 375 persons, how many successful steel rolling mills were in operation in Indianapolis by 1870?

A. Two.

———————◆———————

Q. What Indiana city experienced work stoppages due to the great railroad strikes of 1877?

A. Fort Wayne.

———————◆———————

Q. in 1857 what annual length of school term was adopted by the Indianapolis public school system?

A. Thirty-nine weeks.

Q. Around 1805, what two Shawnee Indian brothers came to the area of present-day Muncie to organize a hostile Indian confederacy?

A. Tecumseh and the Prophet.

Q. Who was the first United States marshal to the Indiana Territory?

A. Robert Hanna.

Q. Who was Indiana's first gubernatorial first lady?

A. Ann Gilmore Hay Jennings.

Q. Who was the only Indiana general killed during the Civil War?

A. Pleasant Hackleman.

Q. In what Indiana city were the first Maxwell touring cars built?

A. New Castle.

Q. What was the removal of the Potawatomi Indians from Indiana to a reservation in Kansas called?

A. "The Trail of Death."

Q. In what year was the construction of the present-day Henry County courthouse begun?

A. 1865.

Q. What presidential campaign slogan carried William Henry Harrison to the White House?

A. "Tippecanoe and Tyler Too."

◆

Q. In November 1986 Dan Quayle was reelected to the Senate by what record-setting portion of votes for a Hoosier senator?

A. Sixty-one percent.

◆

Q. During the 1870s what type of trees started growing out of the tower of the Greensburg Decatur County Courthouse?

A. Aspen.

◆

Q. The 1899 restored West Lafayette mansion that housed the commandant and the state's soldiers after the Civil War was once called by what name?

A. The White House of the Wabash.

◆

Q. In 1934 what notorious criminal escaped from the Lake County Jail in Crown Point by using a fake gun carved of wood?

A. John Dillinger.

◆

Q. Dying on April 4, 1841, how long did William Henry Harrison actually serve as president of the United States?

A. Thirty and one-half days.

Q. Albion-born Earl L. Butz served the nation in what capacity from 1971 to 1976 under Presidents Richard Nixon and Gerald R. Ford?

A. Secretary of Agriculture.

◆

Q. What then little-known car designer accepted the winner's trophy in 1909 for the first major U.S. auto race on the Lake County Courthouse Square at Crown Point?

A. Louis Chevrolet.

◆

Q. Who purchased the Auburn Automobile Company in 1924?

A. Erret Lobban Cord.

◆

Q. What United States Senator from Indiana was a candidate for the 1976 Democratic presidential nomination?

A. Birch E. Bayh, Jr.

◆

Q. Astronaut Virgil I. Grissom graduated from what Indiana institute of higher learning in 1950?

A. Purdue University.

◆

Q. What Lexington-born 1880 Democratic candidate for the vice-presidency of the U.S. was defeated by Republicans Jame A. Garfield and Chester A. Arthur?

A. William H. English.

ARTS & LITERATURE

C H A P T E R F O U R

Q. Where was composer Hoagy Carmichael born in 1899?

A. Bloomington.

---◆---

Q. What hoax Edgar Allan Poe poem, actually penned by Indiana's James Whitcomb Riley, caused a literary uproar across the nation in 1877?

A. "Leonainie."

---◆---

Q. Who was commissioned in 1970 to create an official painting of the State bird of Indiana?

A. Allen L. Hackney.

---◆---

Q. What was Rushville's first newspaper?

A. *Dog-Fennel Gazette.*

---◆---

Q. In 1875 Charles G. Conn began manufacturing what type of musical instruments in Elkhart?

A. Plain brass cornets.

Q. What cartoonist's works are on display at the Wayne County Historical Museum?

A. Gaar Williams.

Q. Where was Indiana essayist and novelist Theodore Dreiser born in 1871?

A. Terre Haute.

Q. In what year did the General Assembly adopt "On the Banks of the Wabash," as the official State song of Indiana?

A. 1913.

Q. The downtown area of what Indiana city is the site of the Round the Fountain Art Fair?

A. Lafayette.

Q. What Mooresville resident designed the Indiana state flag?

A. Paul Hadley.

Q. Where may Dr. Ted's Musical Marvels be seen?

A. Santa Claus.

Q. Snite Museum of Art and O'Shaughnessy Hall Galleries are on what Indiana college campus?

A. University of Notre Dame.

Q. Where was poet William Herschell born in 1873?

A. Spenser.

◆

Q. What roving printer founded the *Enquirer and Indiana Telegraph*, Brookville's first newspaper?

A. John Scott.

◆

Q. Where in 1811 was the first library established in the Northwest Territory?

A. Madison.

◆

Q. What celebration of the arts is held each summer in South Bend's St. Patrick's Park?

A. Firefly Festival of the Performing Arts.

◆

Q. On June 22, 1922 what award-winning fashion designer was born in Fort Wayne?

A. Bill Blass.

◆

Q. *When Knighthood Was in Flower* and *The Bears of Blue River* were novels by what turn-of-the-century Indiana writer?

A. Charles Major.

◆

Q. What Kendallville poet penned the official State poem, "Indiana"?

A. Arthur Franklin Mapes.

Q. For what humorous satirical work is George Ade best known?

A. "Fables in Slang."

◆

Q. In what Adams County town was Gene Stratton Porter married?

A. Decatur.

◆

Q. The play *Happy Birthday, Wanda June* was written by what Indiana-born novelist?

A. Kurt Vonnegut, Jr.

◆

Q. What Indiana university has the oldest college marching band in continual existence?

A. Notre Dame (since 1845).

◆

Q. Where is the Indiana Renaissance Fair held each June?

A. Muncie.

◆

Q. What book did Indiana-born novelist Lew Wallace pen while serving as minister to Turkey under the Garfield administration?

A. *The Prince of India.*

◆

Q. In what Indiana city did James Whitcomb Riley maintain a home at 528 Lockerbie Street from 1892 to 1916?

A. Indianapolis.

Q. Ceramist and painter Alan K. Patrick was born in what Indiana city on June 16, 1942?

A. Richmond.

Q. For what romantic mystery is Indiana writer Meredith Nicholson best remembered?

A. *The House of a Thousand Candles.*

Q. Short story writer Ambrose Bierce spent part of his youth in what Indiana city?

A. Elkhart.

Q. What noted journalist of the muckraking era was born in Madison?

A. David Graham Phillips.

Q. Who became curator of the Indiana University Art Museum in 1976?

A. Adelheid Medicus Gealt.

Q. Where was songwriter Cole Porter born in the 1890s?

A. Peru.

Q. William Seymour served as editorial cartoonist for what Indiana newspaper from 1951 to 1982?

A. Fort Wayne *News-Sentinel.*

Q. Where in 1804 was the first book published in the Indiana Territory?

A. Vincennes.

◆

Q. What Corydon firm is noted for its manufacture of art glass, paper weights, and related items?

A. Zimmerman Glass Company.

◆

Q. Who created the bronze sculpture, *Christ Teaching*, that is situated at the University of Notre Dame?

A. Harold Reed Langland.

◆

Q. Where was Greencastle painter and printmaker Ray H. French born?

A. Terre Haute.

◆

Q. What English gentleman, painter, and art collector founded Hobart?

A. George Earle.

◆

Q. Where is the Ohio River Arts Festival held each spring?
A. Evansville.

◆

Q. In what city is the Louis A. Warren Lincoln Library and Museum?

A. Fort Wayne.

Q. In what Indiana city did nineteenth-century journalist and short story writer Ambrose Bierce spend his childhood and teen-age years.

A. Elkhart.

◆

Q. What turn-of-the-century light opera singer was a resident of North Manchester?

A. Grace Van Studdiford.

◆

Q. Crawfordsville writer and poet Maurice Thompson penned what historical romance in 1900 built around the George Rogers Clark expedition?

A. *Alice of Old Vincennes.*

◆

Q. What water colorist was born in Michigan City on December 25, 1908?

A. Gertrude Felton Harbart.

◆

Q. Composer Van Denman Thompson, who create such works for organ as "Album Leaf," "To Patience," and "Woodland Sketches," was professor of organ and composition at what Indiana college during the first half of the twentieth century?

A. DePauw.

◆

Q. The Clowes Pavilion is a part of what Indiana art museum?

A. Indianapolis Museum of Art.

Q. Where was contemporary artist Robert Indiana born in 1928?

A. New Castle.

Q. Who established the Indianapolis *News* in 1869?

A. John Hilliday.

Q. Where was the popular nineteenth-century song, "I'll Take You Home Again, Kathleen," first performed?

A. Indiana Boys' School, Plainfield.

Q. The Hilton U. Brown Theatre may be found on what Indiana college campus?

A. Butler University.

Q. Two novels by LeRoy MacLeod, *The Years of Peace* and *The Crowded Hill*, are set in what area of Indiana?

A. Wabash Valley.

Q. A fiddler's contest, antique show, and demonstrations of arts and crafts are all a part of what celebration held each fall in Huntington?

A. Forks of the Wabash Pioneer Festival.

Q. Where may one tour the Art Chemical Products Company and observe the manufacture of modeling clay?

A. Huntington.

Q. Appearing in the Indianapolis *Journal* in 1833, what was the first poem of significance to be published in Indiana?

A. "The Hoosier's Nest."

Q. What noted historian from Indiana co-authored, with his wife, *The Rise of American Civilization*?

A. Charles Austin Beard.

Q. For what first work did Indiana-born playwright William Vaughn Moody become best known?

A. *The Great Divide*.

Q. What was the actual name of Liberty-born poet and dramatist Joaquin Miller?

A. Cincinnatus Heine.

Q. A copy of Cyrus Dallin's famous sculpture, *Appeal to the Great Spirit*, may be seen in what Indiana city?

A. Muncie.

Q. At what site near Nappanee is the Pletcher Village Art Festival held?

A. Amish Acres.

Q. Though brought up in New Albany, where was playwright William Vaughn Moody born?

A. Spencer.

Q. The Limberlost Swamp area, made famous by novelist Gene Stratton Porter, was named for what local character?

A. "Limber Jim" McDowell.

---◆---

Q. Where was the first paper mill in the Indiana Territory established in the 1820s?

A. Madison.

---◆---

Q. *The Lost Dutchman Mine: A Short Story to A Tall Tail, Survival in the Wilds*, and *Trails to Hoosier Heritage* were penned by what Hammond-born writer?

A. Harry George Black.

---◆---

Q. What 1845 weekly became the first publication in Indiana to be devoted wholly to local news and literary works?

A. *The Locomotive* (Indianapolis).

---◆---

Q. What novel by Indiana-born writer Edward Eggleston who was first published in France in 1871, had a significant impact on American fiction?

A. *The Hoosier Schoolmaster.*

---◆---

Q. In 1978 what Hoosier potter received the Indiana Potters Guild Special Clay Award?

A. Thomas Marsh.

Q. What are the two best-known novels by Gene Stratton Porter?

A. *Freckles* and *The Girl of the Limberlost*.

Q. Who was "Little Orphan Annie" of the James Whitcomb Riley poem?

A. Annie Gray.

Q. What 1925 work by Indiana writer Theodore Dreiser brought him to the forefront of American realistic fiction?

A. *An American Tragedy*.

Q. When was the first theatrical performance gven in Indianapolis, at Carter's Tavern?

A. December 8, 1823.

Q. For what biographical work did Indiana writer Albert J. Beveridge receive a Pulitzer Prize in 1920?

A. *John Marshall*.

Q. What English painter who came to Indiana in 1837 became known for his studies of Indians and landscapes along the Wabash River?

A. George Winter.

Q. Where was Indiana poet John Hay born in 1838?

A. Salem.

Q. What play by Robert Dale Owen was popular in Indiana during the late 1830s?

A. *Pocahontas.*

◆

Q. Of what Indiana journalist did Will Rogers quip, "No man within our generation was within a mile of him"?

A. Frank McKinney ("Kin") Hubbard.

◆

Q. What theater was opened in Indianapolis in 1854–55 by stage performer and promoter "Yankee" Robinson?

A. The Athenaeum.

◆

Q. In 1983 what Indiana-born writer produced the book entitled *The Mount St. Helen Disaster*?

A. Thomas Gibbons Aylesworth.

◆

Q. What was the title of Lew Wallace's autobiography?

A. *The Wooing of Walkatoon.*

◆

Q. In what year was the Art Association of Indianapolis organized?

A. 1883.

◆

Q. What Indiana-born composer penned such classics as "Star Dust," "Lazybones," "Heart and Soul," and "Georgia On My Mind"?

A. Hoagy Carmichael.

Q. What Indiana writer produced the novel *Brewster's Millions* in 1903?

A. George Barr McCutcheon.

◆

Q. Dillsboro-born painter and illustrator William Harold Zimmerman is best known for what subject matter in his works?

A. Waterfowl.

◆

Q. Indiana painter Clyde Lingle Gilbert was born in what community?

A. Medora.

◆

Q. Under what name was the nation's first wind instrument manufacturing firm established in Elkhart in 1875?

A. Conn & Dupont Company.

◆

Q. What founder of Crown Point became the agricultural editor of the New York *Tribune* in 1849?

A. Solon Robinson.

◆

Q. Where was Indiana author, humorist, and playwright George Ade born in 1866?

A. Near Kentland.

◆

Q. In 1831 what long-lived newspaper opened in Richmond?

A. Richmond *Palladium*.

Q. Where was Indiana novelist Newton Booth Tarkington born in 1869?

A. Indianapolis.

Q. Indianapolis-born sculptor Anthony Joseph Lauck was commissioned to create what 1963 limestone work at the University of Notre Dame?

A. *Our Lady of the University.*

Q. What professor of art at Indiana State University from 1946 to 1973 was born in Richmond?

A. Elmer Johnson Porter.

Q. Thomas Gibbons Aylesworth, who wrote *The Story of Dragons and Other Mythical Monster* and *Science Looks at Mythical Monsters*, was born in what Indiana city?

A. Valparaiso.

Q. Who was named Poet Laureate by the Indiana State Federation of Poetry Clubs for 1980–81?

A. Glenna Glee Jenkins.

Q. *The Man Who Loved Cat Dancing*, *Dutch Uncle*, and *Flambard's Confession* are all novels by what Evansville-born author?

A. Marilyn Jean (Wall) Durham.

Q. Martin John Radecki, who became chief conservator at the Indianapolis Museum of Art in 1975, was born in what Indiana city?

A. South Bend.

◆

Q. What was artist Robert Indiana's original name?

A. Robert Clark.

◆

Q. What Indiana poet wrote "Jim Bludsoe" and "Little Britches"?

A. John Hay.

◆

Q. What impressive facility built in Jonesboro in 1866 was for many years host to popular traveling theatrical companies?

A. The Knights of Pythias Building.

◆

Q. Who was conductor of the Indiana State symphony orchestra from 1930 to 1936?

A. Ferdinand Shaefer.

◆

Q. By 1860, how many weekly and daily newspapers were being published in Indiana?

A. 167.

◆

Q. In what Indiana town was novelist Lew Wallace born in 1827?

A. Brookville.

Q. The scenery along the Blue River just east of Knightstown inspired William Herchell to write what poem?

A. "Ain't God Good to Indiana?".

Q. Later known by such names as the Park, Strand, and Capitol, what theater was opened in Indianapolis in September 1858?

A. Metropolitan Theater.

Q. *The College Widow, The Country Chairman,* and *The Fair Co-ed* are works by what Indiana playwright and humorist?

A. George Ade.

Q. What was David Graham Phillips best-known novel?

A. *Susan Lenox: Her Fall and Rise.*

Q. In what community did Gene Stratton Porter live from 1893 to 1913, where she produced some of her most famous works?

A. Geneva.

Q. What Russian immigrant who came to Indianapolis in 1882 played a major role in the development of music within the state during the late 1800s and early 1900s?

A. Alexander Ernestinoff.

Q. What turn-of-the-century songwriter composed "Hymn to Indiana"?

A. Charles Diven Campbell.

◆

Q. Indiana pioneer poet John Finley was a longtime resident of what county?

A. Wayne.

◆

Q. Frank Mckinney ("Kin") Hubbard, Indianapolis *News* writer and artist of the early twentieth century, created what Hoosier character?

A. Abe Martin.

◆

Q. Published in 1899, what was Newton Booth Tarkington's first novel?

A. *The Gentleman from Indiana.*

◆

Q. Hillsboro-born painter Harry Allen Davis produced what Brazil mural?

A. *History of Clay County.*

◆

Q. What noted collector and art patron was born in Indianapolis in 1904?

A. Harrison Eiteljorg.

◆

Q. Where is Chautauqua of the Arts held?

A. Madison.

Q. What toe-tappin' event is held each summer at the Tippecanoe Battlefield County Park?

A. Fiddlers' Gathering.

———◆———

Q. In 1928 what became Cole Porter's first Broadway success?

A. *Paris*.

———◆———

Q. What Brown County establishment sponsors the Wine & Craft Festival each October?

A. Possum Trot Vineyards.

———◆———

Q. How old was Cole Porter when he had his first song published?

A. Eleven years old.

———◆———

Q. James Whitcomb Riley was born in what Indiana town in 1849?

A. Greenfield.

———◆———

Q. What arts celebration is held the last weekend in June at Layfayette?

A. Midsummer Arts Festival.

———◆———

Q. In 1822 what became the first newspaper to serve Indianapolis?

A. Indianapolis *Gazette*.

Q. Where is Paul Dresser said to have composed his "On the Banks of the Wabash?"

A. West Baden Springs Hotel.

◆

Q. What fine arts librarian and instructor was born in Indianapolis on July 13, 1943?

A. Betty Jo Irvine.

◆

Q. The Marion Coliseum is the site of what annual Easter presentation?

A. Marion Easter Pageant.

◆

Q. Sculptor Jacquard became professor of sculpture at what Hoosier college in 1975?

A. Indiana University.

◆

Q. Where was the first newspaper established in the Indiana Territory in 1804?

A. Vincennes.

◆

Q. What Whig newspaper was founded in Columbus in 1848?

A. *Spirit of the West.*

◆

Q. Noted potter and ceramist Thomas Marsh maintains a studio in what Indiana town?

A. Borden.

Q. Published in 1883, what was James Whitcomb Riley's first collection of works?

A. *The Old Swinnin' Hole and 'Leven More Poems.*

——————◆——————

Q. Water colorist Peggy Ann Brown was born in what Indiana city in 1934?

A. Fort Wayne.

——————◆——————

Q. Experiences during the Mexican War led Lew Wallace to write what 1873 novel?

A. *The Fair God.*

——————◆——————

Q. What University of Evansville art instructor received the Hoosier Salon Merit Award in 1965?

A. Marvin Eisenberg.

——————◆——————

Q. In what year did the Grand Opera House open in Indianapolis?

A. 1875.

——————◆——————

Q. During the Civil War period, who was the most prominent art figure in Indianapolis?

A. Jacob Cox.

——————◆——————

Q. Fort Wayne-born artist Maurice Anthony Papier became the head of what Indiana college's art department in 1972?

A. St. Francis College.

Q. The first clarinet made of metal was patented in what Indiana city on August 27, 1889?

A. Elkhart.

◆

Q. In what state was Indiana author Gene Stratton Porter killed in an automobile accident in 1924?

A. California.

◆

Q. What covered open-air theater is situated in Fort Wayne's Franke Park?

A. Foellinger Theatre.

◆

Q. In what Orange County community may one tour the Kimball Piano & Organ Company's Piano Division plant?

A. French Lick.

◆

Q. What was the first newspaper to be established in the Indiana Territory?

A. *Indiana Gazette* (1804).

◆

Q. Where is the James Whitcomb Riley Festival held each October?

A. Greenfield.

◆

Q. Indiana painter Allen L. Hackney was born in what city?

A. Madison.

Q. In what year was the Indianapolis Dramatic Society formed?

A. 1872.

———◆———

Q. What play was adapted from Indiana author Frederick Landis's *The Glory of His Country*?

A. *The Copperhead.*

———◆———

Q. What 1880 Indianapolis theater hosted such stage greats as Sarah Bernhardt, Edwin Booth, John Drew, and Ethel Barrymore?

A. English Opera House.

———◆———

Q. What artist created the murals for the George Rogers Clark Memorial at Vincennes?

A. Ezra Winter.

———◆———

Q. In 1900 what first novel by Indiana author Theodore Dreiser was suppressed for some time in the United States due to its portrayal of prostitution?

A. *Sister Carrie.*

———◆———

Q. The first art school in Indianapolis was organized in 1877 by what two artists?

A. James R. Gookins and John Love.

———◆———

Q. What was Hoagy Carmichael's actual first name?

A. Hoagland.

ARTS & LITERATURE

Q. What Indiana-born artist is best known for his 1960s Pop Art stenciled inscriptions?

A. Robert Indiana.

------◆------

Q. Associated with both Purdue University and Indiana University, what writer is known as "Indiana Bob"?

A. Robert Lee Novak.

------◆------

Q. Approximately what proportion of the nation's band instruments are manufactured in Elkhart?

A. Fifty percent.

------◆------

Q. The 1981 novel, *Brave Men All*, was written by what Bremen-born author?

A. Nobel Paul Roth.

------◆------

Q. What work stands as Lew Wallace's most popular novel?

A. *Ben Hur.*

------◆------

Q. Where is the Blue River Valley Pioneer Craft Fair held the first weekend in October?

A. Shelbyville.

------◆------

Q. For what two books did Indiana author Newton Booth Tarkington receive Pulitzer Prizes?

A. *The Magnificent Ambersons* (1919) and *Alice Adams* (1922).

------◆------

Q. Where was novelist Edward Eggleston born in 1837?

A. Vevay.

Q. The Wagon Wheel Playhouse is just east of what Indiana city?

A. Warsaw.

———◆———

Q. What northern Hendricks County town became the focus for one of James Whitcomb Riley's poems?

A. Lizton ("A Lizton Humorist").

———◆———

Q. Organized in 1840, what was the first amateur theatrical group in Indianapolis?

A. The Thespians.

———◆———

Q. In what year was the first saxophone manufactured in Elkhart?

A. 1888.

———◆———

Q. Due to strong public prejudice against theatrical productions, what was the first year that the Indianapolis *Journal* finally allowed the advertising of such events in its publications?

A. 1851.

———◆———

Q. Pulitzer Prize-winning editoral cartoonist Charles George Werner joined the staff of what Indiana newspaper in 1947?

A. Indianapolis *Star*.

———◆———

Q. The International Culture Festival is a part of what Indiana city's fall activities?

A. Hammond.

SPORTS & LEISURE
C H A P T E R   F I V E

Q. What type of automobile won the first Indianapolis 500?

A. Marmon "Wasp."

◆

Q. In what year was Indiana University football first televised?

A. 1951 (against Ohio State).

◆

Q. The Indiana state championship for fire department hose and engine maneuvers was won in both 1882 and 1887 by what town?

A. Bremen.

◆

Q. What water event is held on West Fork Whitewater River between Laurel and Brookville each September?

A. The Whitewater Canoe Race.

◆

Q. On what date was the nation's first night baseball game played at the old League Park in Fort Wayne?

A. Saturday, June 2, 1883.

Q. What Franklin native was the first Milwaukee Buck to play in an All-Star game?

A. Jon McGlocklin (1969).

———◆———

Q. How many times did Indiana-born pitcher Carl Erskine help the Brooklyn Dodgers to win the National League pennant?

A. Five.

———◆———

Q. What Livonia-born individual coached at Carleton, Indiana, and Stanford, 1922–51?

A. Everett Dean.

———◆———

Q. Where is the Mad Anthony Celebrity Golf Tournament held?

A. Fort Wayne.

———◆———

Q. What Lebanon-born basketball guard was the first prep athlete to be featured on the cover of *Sports Illustrated*?

A. Rick Mount.

———◆———

Q. Muncie native Don Odle earned his 300th basketball coaching victory in 1967 at what Indiana college?

A. Taylor.

———◆———

Q. What was the winning time of the first Indianapolis 500?

A. 6 hours, 41 minutes, and 8 seconds.

Q. What Major League player was born and died in Madison?

A. Tommy Thevenow.

———◆———

Q. What was Indiana-born Major League pitcher "Three Finger" Brown's actual name?

A. Mordecai Peter Brown.

———◆———

Q. Where did pitcher Tommy John attend college?

A. Indiana State College.

———◆———

Q. John Wooden, legendary basketball coach, graduated from what Indiana university?

A. Purdue.

———◆———

Q. Butler, DePauw, Franklin, Indiana, Purdue, and Wabash universities formed what sports organization on March 1, 1890?

A. Indiana Intercollegiate Athletic Association.

———◆———

Q. What sport was officially banned by the faculty at Indiana State University from 1908 to 1919?

A. Football.

———◆———

Q. Who coached Indiana State University football from 1957 to 1965?

A. Bill Jones.

Q. Who was Notre Dame's first paid football coach?

A. Frank Hering.

---◆---

Q. In what Indiana city are Louisville Slugger baseball bats and Power Bilt golf clubs manufactured?

A. Jeffersonville (by Hillerich & Bradsby Company).

---◆---

Q. What Kokomo-born basketball guard was known as "Splendid Splinter"?

A. Jim Rayl.

---◆---

Q. Eddie Roush, who played for such teams as the White Sox, Giants, and Reds, was born in what Indiana town in 1893?

A. Oakland City.

---◆---

Q. How many seasons did Martinsville native John Wooden coach the UCLA Bruins?

A. Twenty-five (1949–73).

---◆---

Q. Where were the bricks used to pave the Indianapolis Motor Speedway manufactured?

A. Veedersburg.

---◆---

Q. In what year was Indiana-born major leaguer Max Carey inducted into the Baseball Hall of Fame?

A. 1961.

Q. All-American honors went to what Indiana University football player in 1986?

A. Van Waiters.

———◆———

Q. Where is the Feast of the Hunters' Moon celebration held each October?

A. Fort Ouiatenon (near West Lafayette).

———◆———

Q. What racing event is held on Memorial Day weekend at the Anderson Speedway?

A. The "Little 500."

———◆———

Q. In what structure was the first Notre Dame varsity basketball game played?

A. The gymnasium of Carroll Hall.

———◆———

Q. What ski facility is west of La Porte?

A. Ski Valley.

———◆———

Q. The Indiana Football Hall of Fame, established in 1974, is an affiliation of what sports organization?

A. Indiana Football Coaches Association.

———◆———

Q. What Notre Dame athlete in 1964–65 became the school's first sportsman in nineteen years to win letters in three different sports in one school year?

A. Kevin Hardy (football, basketball and baseball).

Q. Who were the two head coaches of the Indianapolis Jets during the 1948–49 season.

A. Bruce Hale and Burl Fiddle.

◆

Q. What Indiana quarterback was named the Big Ten's Most Valuable Player in 1979?

A. Tim Clifford.

◆

Q. Where is the Circus City Festival held each July?

A. Peru.

◆

Q. What Indiana University basketball player, called "The Baby Bull," dropped out of school two years early to join the Indiana Pacers for the 1971–72 season?

A. George McGinnis.

◆

Q. In what year was the first Indianapolis 500 run?

A. 1911.

◆

Q. Indiana-born pitcher Carl Erskine struck out how many Yankees, including Mickey Mantle, in the third game of the 1953 World Series?

A. Fourteen.

◆

Q. What special event, built around an 1890s theme, is enjoyed in Anderson during the second weekend in June?

A. Gaslight Festival.

Q. What facility is the home of Butler University basketball?

A. Hinkle Fieldhouse.

◆

Q. What basketball player received the first full women's athletic scholarship at Purdue University?

A. Sue Fackler.

◆

Q. On October 8, 1956, what Indiana-born baseball player became the first person to pitch a perfect game in a World Series?

A. Don Larsen.

◆

Q. Where is the International Palace Sports Hall of Fame?

A. North Webster.

◆

Q. Who coached the Purdue football team to a no-lose season in both 1891 and 1892?

A. Knowlton ("Snake") Ames.

◆

Q. What Indiana-born baseball player is considered to be the best player to come out of the Federal League?

A. Edd J. ("Eddie") Roush.

◆

Q. Where is the Steuben County 101 Lakes Festival held each June?

A. Angola.

Q. What team represented Indiana in the nation's first night baseball game?

A. Students from Fort Wayne Methodist Episcopal College.

———◆———

Q. What Notre Dame basketball player set a season record for rebounds in 1957–58 at 499?

A. Tom Hawkins.

———◆———

Q. Where is the Fayette County Free Fair held in early August?

A. Connersville.

———◆———

Q. What famous Notre Dame passing–receiving twosome of the 1960s were known as Mr. Fling and Mr. Cling?

A. Terry Hanratty and Jim Seymour.

———◆———

Q. On October 27, 1900, what Purdue quarterback kicked seven field goals against Rose Poly in Lafayette.

A. E. C. ("Little Robbie") Robertson.

———◆———

Q. How long is the oval track at the Indianapolis Motor Speedway?

A. Two and one-half miles.

———◆———

Q. What holiday event is held the first and second weekends of December at Hillforest in Aurora?

A. Victorian Christmas.

Q. What Hedrick-born basketball player became Purdue's fourth All-American, 1937–38?

A. Jewell Young.

———◆———

Q. Noted for his blazing fast ball, where was "Babe" Adams born in the 1880s?

A. Tipton.

———◆———

Q. What is the nickname of the Indiana State University teams?

A. "Sycamores."

———◆———

Q. Where are the U.S. Open Clay Court Tennis Championships held each spring?

A. Indianapolis Sports Center.

———◆———

Q. What three Notre Dame Heisman Trophy winners also participated in Irish basketball?

A. John Lattner (1951–52), John Lujack (1943–44), and Paul Hornung (1954–55).

———◆———

Q. Goshen is the site of what October celebration?

A. Sunflower Festival.

———◆———

Q. What football player set a Indiana University career record for total points scored?

A. Jade Butcher (180).

Q. What Purdue four-letter athlete born in New Ross was selected to the Indiana High School Silver Anniversary All-State Team in 1970?

A. Howard Williams.

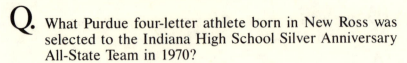

Q. What South Bend native captained the UCLA Bruins his junior and senior years (1967, 1968) when they recorded a win-loss record of 59–1?

A. Mike Warren.

Q. In 1984 linebacker Ed Martin of Indiana State was the seventh round draft choice of what NFL club?

A. Dallas Cowboys.

Q. What Indiana State football player was named the Missouri Valley Conference "Defensive Player of the Year" in 1984?

A. Wayne Davis.

Q. Prior to becoming head football coach, Knute Rockne served Notre Dame University in what bivocational capacity?

A. Assistant football coach and chemistry instructor.

Q. Through the 1988–89 season, Bobby Knight has led the Indiana Hoosiers to how many Big ten basketball championships?

A. Nine.

Q. In what year did the Pistons leave Fort Wayne and relocate in Detroit, Michigan?

A. 1958.

———◆———

Q. Holland-born Don Buse played guard for what college basketball team?

A. University of Evansville.

———◆———

Q. McDonald's Open Tennis Tournament is a part of what Tell City celebration?

A. Schweizer Fest.

———◆———

Q. What Anderson-born basketball coach was known as the "Old Gray Fox"?

A. Everett Case.

———◆———

Q. February 21, 1970, basketball player Austin Carr set a Notre Dame single game scoring record in the Coliseum with how many points?

A. Fifty-five.

———◆———

Q. What Notre Dame player holds the school's record in total offense yards (2,813) in a single season?

A. Joe Theismann (1970).

———◆———

Q. What celebration is held in Corydon each year during the second week of May?

A. Popcorn Festival.

Q. How many baseball players were drafted by the major leagues from Indiana State Universtiy in 1987?

A. Eight.

———◆———

Q. What is the seating capacity of Indiana University's Memorial Stadium?

A. 52,354.

———◆———

Q. Scenic excursion trips aboard a 1900s steam train may be enjoyed on what railroad line at Connersville?

A. Whitewater Valley Railroad.

———◆———

Q. What Irish quarterback established a career passing record for most completions?

A. Steve Beuerlein (473).

———◆———

Q. Where is the Little 500 Bicycle Race held each spring?

A. Indiana University campus, Bloomington.

———◆———

Q. What football trophy is presented the winner of the traditional Indiana vs. Purdue game?

A. Old Oaken Bucket.

———◆———

Q. The Labor Day weekend Jail "Breakout" is held in what Indiana town?

A. Crawfordsville.

Q. In 1977 who became the first driver to win the Indianapolis 500 four times?

A. A. J. Foyt.

———◆———

Q. What Purdue baseball player caught the last out made by Joe Dimaggio?

A. Felix Mackiewicz.

———◆———

Q. In what year did the Colts relocate from Baltimore to Indianapolis?

A. 1984.

———◆———

Q. What Lebanon native was a catcher for two years for the Washington Senators?

A. Joe McCabe.

———◆———

Q. Steam Harvest Days is a Labor Day celebration in what Indiana community?

A. Rockville.

———◆———

Q. Where is the home of the Indiana Football Hall of Fame?

A. Richmond.

———◆———

Q. In the summer before his freshman year at Notre Dame, Marc Kelly played in what movie that temporarily cost him his amateur status with the NCAA?

A. *Fast Break.*

Q. What South Bend-born Indiana University basketball player held the most Big Ten Conference marks when he graduated in 1955?

A. Don Schlundt.

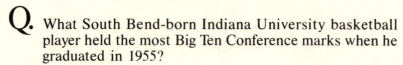

Q. In 1922 Converse Rubber Company, of basketball shoe fame, was founded by what Columbus-born athlete and sports promoter?

A. Charles ("Chuck") Taylor.

Q. What Indiana-born Major Leaguer was inducted into the Baseball Hall of Fame in 1963?

A. Edgar C. ("Sam") Rice.

Q. The UCLA Bruins earned how many straight wins, 1970–73, under the coaching of Indiana native John Wooden?

A. Seventy-five.

Q. What water race is held the third weekend in April, starting at Lake Holiday via Crawfordsville and ending at Deer Mill?

A. Sugar Creek Canoe Race.

Q. In mid-June what event is held at the Lane Place in Crawfordsville?

A. Strawberry Festival.

Q. What basketball great paced Roosevelt High School, East Chicago, to a 28–0 season and an Indiana State championship in 1970?

A. Jim Bradley.

Q. Where did Indianapolis-born Chuck Klein get his start in pro baseball?

A. Evansville, III League.

Q. In what year was the Harrison County Fair first held?
A. 1860.

Q. For what season did Larry Bird receive the Missouri Valley Conference Player of the Year award?

A. 1977–78.

Q. In what year did Gene Keady become head basketball coach at Purdue?

A. 1981.

Q. What is the major attraction for ski buffs in Orange County?

A. Paoli Peaks Ski Area.

Q. What University of Evansville basketball coach had his best season in 1965, compiling a 29–0 mark?

A. Arad McCutchan.

Q. What All-State basketball player from Arsenal Technical High, Indianapolis was known as "Houdini of the Hardwood"?

A. John Townsend.

———◆———

Q. In 1921 V. B. Brown, A. E. Byrnes, and G. P. Weatherton became the first Purdue students to compete in what intercollegiate sport?

A. Golf.

———◆———

Q. What celebration, built around a railroad theme, is held in Logansport?

A. Iron Horse Festival.

———◆———

Q. Where was the great harness race horse Dan Patch foaled in December 1896?

A. Oxford.

———◆———

Q. What is the trophy presented to the winning team of the annual football game between Notre Dame and Purdue?

A. The "Shillelagh."

———◆———

Q. How many Notre Dame coaches have been elected to the National Football Foundation Hall of Fame?

A. Five: Jesse Harper, Knute Rockne, Frank Leahy, Ara Parseghian, and Dan Devine.

Q. In April 1913 who became the first woman to be officially banned as a participant in the Indianapolis 500?

A. Vivian Prescott.

———————◆———————

Q. In 1979 Larry Bird set an Indiana State University game record with how many rebounds against Southern Illinois?

A. Nineteen.

———————◆———————

Q. What was the first year for Indiana State University to enter into intercollegiate football?

A. 1889 (against DePauw).

———————◆———————

Q. In addition to the assistant coach and the team trainer, how many members of the Purdue football team were killed in a train wreck in Indianapolis on October 31, 1903?

A. Thirteen.

———————◆———————

Q. The "Old Oaken Bucket" trophy of Indiana and Purdue football rivalry came from what location in southern Indiana?

A. Bruner Farm (between Kent and Hanover).

———————◆———————

Q. During the 1953–54 season, what Notre Dame basketball player became the first Irish player to average more than twenty points a game?

A. Dick Rosenthal.

Q. What two Irishmen co-captained the Notre Dame basketball team during the 1978–79 season?

A. Bruce Flowers and Bill Laimbeer.

———◆———

Q. Deaf mute Albert Berg was the first football coach of what Indiana university?

A. Purdue.

———◆———

Q. What late-July Muncie celebration features special events, amusement rides, and tours of the Kerr Glass plant?

A. Glass Days Festival.

———◆———

Q. What ski facility is just southwest of Nashville?

A. Ski World Ski Resort.

———◆———

Q. How many spectators were present at the running of the first Indianapolis 500?

A. Over 80,000.

———◆———

Q. What theme park is near Santa Claus?

A. Holiday World.

———◆———

Q. What school was the first opponent Purdue faced in intercollegiate play?

A. Butler.

Q. In 1889 what school christened the Purdue football team with the nickname, "Boilermakers"?

A. Wabash.

———◆———

Q. A large collection of high school memorabilia may be viewed at what Indianapolis facility?

A. Indiana Basketball Hall of Fame.

———◆———

Q. What sportswriter was responsible for immortalizing the Four Horsemen of Notre Dame?

A. Grantland Rice.

———◆———

Q. Hot air balloon races, fireworks, chili cook-off, and hydroplane racing are all a part of what summer event in Evansville?

A. Freedom Festival.

———◆———

Q. What three years did Wilbur Shaw win the Indianapolis 500?

A. 1937, 1939, and 1940.

———◆———

Q. Who holds the Notre Dame record for pass receptions in a career?

A. Tom Gatewood (157).

———◆———

Q. What are the colors of Indiana State University teams?

A. Blue and White.

Q. Archer Park in Fort Wayne is the site of what September celebration?-

A. Johnny Appleseed Festival.

◆

Q. What 61,000-seat facility is the home of the Indianapolis Colts?

A. Hoosier Dome.

◆

Q. Where are such sprint car racing events as the "Tony Hulman Classic" and the "Hot Hundred Midgets" held?

A. Terre Haute Action Track.

◆

Q. The National Track and Field Hall of Fame is in what Indiana city?

A. Indianapolis.

◆

Q. In what Indiana city is the Little Red Schoolhouse Festival held?

A. Hammond.

◆

Q. Who was named Notre Dame's first Walter Camp All-American?

A. George Gipp (1920).

◆

Q. Indiana State University is affiliated with what basketball conference?

A. Missouri Valley.

Q. Who was named general manager of the Indianapolis Colts on April 26, 1984?

A. Jim Irsay.

———◆———

Q. The Little Italy Festival is held in what Parke County town on Labor Day weekend?

A. Clinton.

———◆———

Q. During the January 2, 1989 Fiesta Bowl, what Notre Dame quarterback completed 7 of 11 passes for a total of 213 yards and 2 touchdowns?

A. Tony Rice.

———◆———

Q. Who did the Indiana Hoosiers defeat in a 34–10 victory at the Liberty Bowl on December 28, 1988?

A. South Carolina Gamecocks.

———◆———

Q. What Notre Dame flanker in 1987 became the fifty-third Heisman Trophy winner?

A. Tim Brown.

———◆———

Q. Who coached Purdue's first basketball team in 1896?

A. F. Homer Curtis.

———◆———

Q. By what nickname was Hoosier major league player Max Carey called?

A. "Scoops."

Q. On October 31, 1988, what team did the Indianapolis Colts defeat 55–23, in the first "Monday Night Football" game to be broadcast from the Hoosier Dome?

A. Denver Broncos.

Q. In what year did the Fort Wayne Pistons join the National Basketball League?

A. 1941.

Q. What Notre Dame basketball player holds the career rebounding average record with 16.9?

A. Walt Sahm (1962–65).

Q. The Indianapolis Indians are at home in what facility?

A. Bush Stadium.

Q. The Indiana Pacers were a members of what pro basketball league from 1967 to 1976?

A. American Basketball Association.

Q. When was Notre Dame's first ever 12–0 football season?

A. 1988.

Q. Born in Gary, what individual became head coach and physical education instructor at Duke University from 1960–69?

A. Vic Bubas.

Q. What Indiana city holds an Italian Festival, Serb Festival, and Greek Festival each summer?

A. Merrillville.

———◆———

Q. How many national football championships has Notre Dame won?

A. Eight.

———◆———

Q. During the 1969–70 season, what Indiana Pacers player came in second in the ABA for most rebounds?

A. Mel Daniels (with 1,462).

———◆———

Q. In 1887 who became the first Purdue football player to score points in intercollegiate play?

A. J. M. Sholl (Scholl).

———◆———

Q. What trophy is passed back and forth between Indiana University and the University of Kentucky in football competition?

A. The "Bourbon Barrel."

———◆———

Q. Who won the first Indianapolis 500?

A. Ray Harroun.

———◆———

Q. At the end of spring football practice, what award is presented to the top Notre Dame player at each position?

A. Hering Award.

Q. What Princeton-born baseball figure managed the New York Mets to their 1969 World Series victory over the Baltimore Orioles?

A. Gil Hodges.

◆

Q. What award is presented to the most valuable player of the annual Notre Dame–Kentucky basketball game?

A. The Shively Memorial Plaque.

◆

Q. In 1929 what two Boilermakers became the first Purdue football players to be named All-American?

A. Elmer Sleight and Ralph Welch.

◆

Q. Where is the Orange County Pumpkin Festival held?

A. French Lick.

◆

Q. Before joining the major leagues, Bernie Allen played what position for three years at Purdue?

A. Shortstop.

◆

Q. Notre Dame walk-on Mike Oriard, who served as co-captain of the 1969 team, played for what NFL franchise?

A. Kansas City Chiefs.

◆

Q. Market Square Area is the home of what hockey team?

A. Indianapolis Checkers.

Q. What high school basketball star was known as "Muncie Mortar"?

A. Ron Bonham.

Q. Who was the owner of the Fort Wayne Pistons?

A. Fred Zollner.

Q. What years did Knute Rockne serve as head football coach at Notre Dame?

A. 1918 to 1931.

Q. East Chicago-born Vince Boryla played for what NBA team from 1950 to 1954?

A. New York Knicks.

Q. How many hits did Hoosier Tommy Thevenow get while playing against the Yankees in the 1926 World Series?

A. Ten.

Q. Notre Dame defeated what opponent, 19–18, in the 1983 Liberty Bowl?

A. Boston College.

Q. How many games did Indiana-born pitcher "Babe" Adams win against such Detroit Tigers during the 1909 World Series?

A. Three.

Q. What Indiana State basketball player was named "NCAA Player of the Year" in 1979?

A. Larry Bird.

———◆———

Q. On January 28, 1985, who replaced Hal Hunter as head coach of the Indianapolis Colts?

A. Rod Dowhower.

———◆———

Q. By what other nickname was Hoosier pitcher "Three Finger" Brown called?

A. "Miner."

———◆———

Q. What high school coach led East Chicago Washington to the state crown in 1960?

A. John Baratto.

———◆———

Q. What Evansville native was the top draft pick of the NBA's Chicago Bulls and played two years for the team in 1967 and 1968?

A. Dave Schellhase.

———◆———

Q. Where was 1950s Dodgers pitcher Carl Erskine born?

A. Anderson.

———◆———

Q. NBA–ABA player John Barnhill, born in Evansville, was known by what nickname due to his speed?

A. "Rabbit."

Q. What was the full name of Indiana-born Major League pitcher "Babe" Adams?

A. Charles Benjamin Adams.

———◆———

Q. From what source did the University of Evansville teams receive the nickname, "Aces""

A. Initials of American College of Evansville.

———◆———

Q. What type of boats are featured in the Governor's Cup Race on the Ohio River at Madison?

A. Hydroplanes.

———◆———

Q. What are Purdue's team colors?

A. Gold and black.

———◆———

Q. In the history of Notre Dame basketball, what player ranks second in career scoring?

A. Adrian Dantley.

———◆———

Q. What is the only man-made whitewater raceway in North America?

A. East Race Waterway (downtown South Bend).

———◆———

Q. The Auburn-Cord-Duesenberg Festival featuring a classic car show, auto auction, and parades, is held each Labor Day weekend in what Indiana city?

A. Auburn.

Q. What two Notre Dame players have finished second in the voting for the Heisman Trophy?

A. Angelo Bertelli (1941) and Joe Theismann (1970).

Q. Tommy John was born in what Indiana city on May 22, 1943?

A. Terre Haute.

Q. What special honor was bestowed on Indiana-born player Eddie Roush by the Reds in 1969?

A. Named to all-time Cincinnati team.

Q. Notre Dame was represented in the 1988 Hula Bowl by what three players?

A. Tim Brown, Chuck Lanza, and Brandy Wells.

Q. What All-State Southport High (Indianapolis) basketball guard played for the Kentucky Wildcats, then signed with the ABA Kentucky Colonels?

A. Louie Dampier.

Q. Who ranks as Indiana State's all-time rushing leader?
A. Vincent Allen.

Q. What Notre Dame basketball player was known as "The Ice Man"?

A. Dwight Clay.

Q. What Indiana-born baseball player was known by the nickname "Bubbles"?

A. Eugene Franklin Hargrave.

———◆———

Q. In 1989 the U.S. Basketball Writers Association bestowed "Coach of the Year" honors on what individual?

A. Bobby Knight, Indiana University.

———◆———

Q. Morocco-born baseball player Sam Rice played for what club from 1915 to 1933?

A. Washington Senators.

———◆———

Q. What event is held in late October at Historic Fort Wayne featuring Indians, trappers and traders in period games and exhibitions?

A. Trapper's Rendezvous.

———◆———

Q. In 1962, what five individuals were the first inductees into the Indiana Basketball Hall of Fame?

A. Homer ("Stoney") Stonebraker, Ernest ("Griz") Wagner, Ward ("Piggy") Lambert, Robert ("Fuzzy") Vandivier, and John ("Johnnie") Wooden.

———◆———

Q. What Yorktown native participated on the 1948 U.S. Olympic basketball team and went on to play with the NBA Indianapolis Olympians from 1950 to 1952?

A. Cliff Barker.

Q. What Indiana city is noted for its Three Rivers Festival?

A. Fort Wayne.

———◆———

Q. Following his Indiana State football career, Mike Simmonds signed with what NFL team?

A. Tampa Bay Buccaneers.

———◆———

Q. What Notre Dame basketball player broke a 45-year single game record formerly held by Justin Moloney, scoring 35 points against Loyola in 1953?

A. Joe Bertrand.

———◆———

Q. Who captained the first Purdue football team?

A. J. B. Burris.

———◆———

Q. What Gary-born basketball guard was the star of Tennessee State's three NAIA championship teams, 1957–59?

A. Dick Barnett.

———◆———

Q. What was the first intercollegiate sport to be played at Purdue?

A. Baseball.

———◆———

Q. Who was the Fort Wayne Pistons first coach and geneal manager?

A. Carl Bennett.

Q. The grandstands, paddocks, and bleachers at the Indianapolis Motor Speedway will accommodate how many spectators?

A. 238,000.

———◆———

Q. What three Notre Dame basketball players have been designated three-time consensus All-Americans by the NCAA?

A. Ed ("Moose") Krause (1932–33–34), Paul Nowak (1936–37–38), and John Moir (1936–37–38).

———◆———

Q. At what Jeffersonville facility may one see displays and memorabilia of the riverboat era?

A. Howard Steamboat Museum.

———◆———

Q. Notre Dame played its first football game in what year?
A. 1887.

———◆———

Q. What Indiana State basketball player made the game-winning shot to beat Arkansas in the 1979 Regional finals?

A. Bob Heaton.

———◆———

Q. What four former Indiana State basketball players were drafted by the NBA's Boston Celtics?

A. Duane Klueh, Jerry Newsom, Larry Bird, and Winfred King.

Q. Where was baseball player Max George Carey born on January 11, 1890?

A. Terre Haute.

---◆---

Q. In 1889 what organization stepped in to regulate rules and create an intercollegiate football league in Indiana?

A. Y.M.C.A.

---◆---

Q. What Indiana University football player returned a punt for a touch down against Marquette in 1953?

A. Ron Drzewiecki.

---◆---

Q. Where is the "Thinking of Christmas" celebration held?

A. Historic Billie Creek Village (near Rockville).

---◆---

Q. What Indianapolis-born basketball center was named All-American and Helms Player of the Year while playing for Kentucky in his only varsity season, 1935?

A. Leroy Edwards.

---◆---

Q. Where was Major League pitcher Don Larsen born in 1929?

A. Michigan City.

---◆---

Q. What team did Purdue defeat, 14–13, at the Rose Bowl on January 2, 1967?

A. Southern California.

Q. What Baseball Hall of Famer was born in New Albany on July 7, 1909?

A. Billy Herman.

———————◆———————

Q. Following his basketball career at Purdue, what Bloomfield native once shot the winning point for the West Point Cadets while seated on the floor?

A. Elmer ("Ollie") Oliphant.

———————◆———————

Q. What was the first major league team to sign Indiana-born Gil Hodges?

A. Brooklyn Dodgers.

———————◆———————

Q. A combined demolition derby and harness-racing are just two featured activities at what Blackford County event?

A. The Converse Fair.

———————◆———————

Q. Eugene Franklin Hargrave, who with a .353 average was the National League batting champion for 1926, was born in what Indiana town on July 15, 1892?

A. New Haven.

———————◆———————

Q. Professor Harvey Wiley, who founded the first baseball team at Purdue, went on to become president of what Indiana college?

A. Hanover College.

Q. Terre Haute-born Terry Dischinger, was named Rookie of the Year while playing for what NBA team?

A. Chicago Zephyrs.

———◆———

Q. What New Castle native captained the 1940 Hoosier national basketball championship team?

A. Marv Huffman.

———◆———

Q. Madison native Larry Humes entered the record books as highest scorer during his 1963–65 basketball career at what college?

A. University of Evansville.

———◆———

Q. Tommy John was offered how many college basketball scholarships?

A. Thirty-five.

———◆———

Q. What Pecksburg native began the Indiana high school basketball tournament in 1911?

A. Arthur Trester.

———◆———

Q. What two Hoosiers hold the National League record of four home runs in a single game?

A. Chuck Klein and Gil Hodges.

———◆———

Q. What was Knute Rockne's coaching career record?

A. 105 wins, 12 losses, and 5 ties.

Q. What Terre Haute-born basketball center played for the University of Kansas and received the Helms Player of the Year award in 1952?

A. Clyde Lovellette.

———◆———

Q. What Indianapolis-born twin brothers were both playing and academic All-Americans at Indiana under Branch McCracken?

A. Tom and Dick Van Arsdale.

———◆———

Q. A National League career record of fourteen home runs, with bases loaded, was set by what Indiana-born baseball player?

A. Gil Hodges.

———◆———

Q. Prior to the building of Notre Dame Stadium where did the Irish play football?

A. Cartier Field.

———◆———

Q. What Monrovia native coached eight years at Ball State (1930–37) and twenty-four years at Indiana (1939–43, 1947–65)?

A. Branch McCracken.

———◆———

Q. Who was named "Mr. Basketball" after leading Indianapolis's Washington High to the state title in 1969?

A. George McGinnis.

Q. Who were the legendary Four Horsemen of Notre Dame?

A. Jim Crowley, Elmer Layden, Don Miller, and Harry Stuhldreher.

◆

Q. What is the home court for the Indiana State University basketball team?

A. Hulman Center.

◆

Q. What 1940 Indiana State graduate ranks as the state's all-time winningest high school coach?

A. Howard Sharpe.

◆

Q. In early August, where is the Germania Maennerchor Volkfest held?

A. Evansville.

◆

Q. Where was third baseman-turned-pitcher "Three Finger" Brown born in 1876?

A. Nyesville.

◆

Q. What was the full name of Indiana-born major leaguer Billy Herman?

A. William Jennings Bryan Herman.

◆

Q. Who replaced Clifford Barker as head coach of the Indianapolis Olympians during the 1950–51 season?

A. Wallace Jones.

SCIENCE & NATURE

C H A P T E R   S I X

Q. What was the state flower of Indiana from 1931 to 1957?

A. Zinnia.

———◆———

Q. At an elevation of 192 feet, what is the tallest sand dune in Indiana Dunes State Park?

A. Mount Tom.

———◆———

Q. What Hoosier became the second American in space on July 21, 1961?

A. Virgil Grissom.

———◆———

Q. Under what brand name did Tom Taggart start bottling mineral water at French Lick in 1910?

A. Pluto Water.

———◆———

Q. Devil's Ice Box and Box Canyon are both features of what Indiana state park?

A. Turkey Run State Park.

Q. What state agency oversees quality control in Indiana's milk industry?

A. Creamery License Division.

———◆———

Q. The history and development of interurban transit systems is the subject of what Noblesville attraction?

A. Indiana Transportation Museum.

———◆———

Q. What is New Castle's largest community park?

A. Baker Park.

———◆———

Q. Who served at Purdue as the first State chemist and in 1906 became the first director of the Federal Food and Drug Administration?

A. Harvey Wiley.

———◆———

Q. One of the nation's first electric interurban lines was opened between what two Indiana communities in 1893?

A. Brazil and Harmony.

———◆———

Q. The lumber business in Michigan City handled how many board feet of lumber during its peak year of 1884?

A. 160,000,000.

———◆———

Q. The nation's first gasoline pump was installed in what Indiana city on September 5, 1885?

A. Fort Wayne.

Q. The "germ-free" guinea pig was developed by what University of Notre Dame professor?

A. J. A. Reyniers.

Q. To meet demands created by World War I, how many tons of coal were produced in Indiana during 1918?

A. Over thirty million.

Q. In what Indiana city was the first transistor radio receiver manufactured in 1954?

A. Indianapolis.

Q. Where does Indiana rank among other states in the production of peppermint and spearmint?

A. Fourth.

Q. McBrides Bluffs are along what Indiana river?

A. White.

Q. In what year were Hereford cattle introduced into Indiana?

A. 1871.

Q. What portion of Indiana counties produce sand and gravel?

A. Over two-thirds.

Q. Standing 1,167 feet above sea level, what is the highest point in the southern portion of Indiana?

A. Weedpatch Hill (Brown County).

———◆———

Q. By what name did the Delaware Indians call the Eel River?

A. Shakamak (snakefish).

———◆———

Q. What cliff in Versailles State Park is named for a young medical student, cornered there by irate locals after being found exhuming the body of a prominent citizen for study?

A. Gordon's Leap.

———◆———

Q. Where was Indiana's first astronomical observatory opened in 1861?

A. Earlham College.

———◆———

Q. How many chicken hatcheries are there in Indiana?

A. Twenty-eight.

———◆———

Q. What is Indiana's largest cash crop?

A. Corn.

———◆———

Q. According to the latest agricultural census, what is the age of the average farmer in Indiana?

A. 49.4 years old.

Q. In what year were strawberries first cultivated in southern Indiana?

A. 1887.

———◆———

Q. Situated between Newburgh and Evansville, what is the largest group of prehistoric Indian earthworks in Indiana?

A. Angel Mounds.

———◆———

Q. How many state parks are in Indiana?

A. Nineteen.

———◆———

Q. What Hoosier invented the first mechanically successful clutch-driven, spark-ignition automobile?

A. Elwood Haynes.

———◆———

Q. The fossil remains of what type of prehistoric animals unearthed near Lake Galatia were sent to the Smithsonian Institution and the American Museum of Natural History?

A. Mastodons.

———◆———

Q. What is the incubation period of the cardinal?

A. Twelve to thirteen days.

———◆———

Q. What is the largest lake in Marshall County?

A. Maxinkuckee.

Q. What naturally occurring item was hollowed out to create a mausoleum for the interment of nineteenth-century Bedford doctor Winthrop Foote and his brother, Ziba?

A. A large limestone boulder.

Q. In 1905 what company purchased 6,000 acres of land on the site of present-day Gary to establish the world's second largest fully-integrated steel plant?

A. United States Steel Corporation.

Q. Since 1894, what are the only two years that the amount of land devoted to growing corn in Indiana has dropped below four million acres?

A. 1940 and 1941.

Q. In 1900 what Huntington resident served as a human guinea pig in 1900, for Dr. Walter Reed's yellow fever vaccine experiments in Cuba?

A. John R. Kissinger.

Q. During pioneer days, "Forks of the Rivers" referred to the confluence of what two rivers?

A. Wabash and Little Wabash.

Q. In 1905 what Richmond resident developed a new hybrid rose which he named in honor of his city?

A. E. Gurney Hill.

Q. In 1930, a record production year for Indiana, how many tons of processing cucumbers were harvested in the state?

A. 20,400.

———◆———

Q. With only eight acres of vineyards in Switzerland County in 1810, how many gallons of wine were produced in the county that year?

A. 2,400.

———◆———

Q. What was the approximate combined weight of furs shipped annually from Vincennes and Quiatenon during the early years of the Indiana Territory?

A. 13,000 pounds.

———◆———

Q. Limestone from the Bedford area was used in the construction of what famous New York City skyscraper?

A. Empire State Building.

———◆———

Q. What is the largest natural lake contained completely within Indiana?

A. Lake Wawasee.

———◆———

Q. What Miami Indian chief probably conducted America's first agricultural school sometime between 1795 and 1800?

A. Little Turtle.

Q. The Joseph Moore Museum of Natural Science, featuring both mastodon and allosaurus skeletons, is on the campus of what Indiana college?

A. Earlham College.

◆

Q. What type of tree brought to Indiana from China by William Maclure was first planted at New Harmony?

A. Golden rain tree.

◆

Q. Where was the first Indiana Apple Show held on November 6, 1911?

A. Tomlinson Hall, Indianapolis.

◆

Q. Established in 1916, what became Indiana's first state park?

A. McCormick's State Park.

◆

Q. What synthetic vitamin was first commercially manufactured in Evansville in 1927?

A. Vitamin D.

◆

Q. In 1926 what pest first attacked Indiana peppermint?

A. Flea beetle.

◆

Q. What is the highest glacially produced ridge in northern Indiana?

A. The Valparaiso Moraine.

Q. In the history of corn production in Indiana, what was the first year that state-wide yields reached an average of one hundred bushels per acre?

A. 1969.

———◆———

Q. What became the official state bird of Indiana in 1933?

A. Cardinal.

———◆———

Q. In what year was the first coal mine dug in the Bicknell field?

A. 1875.

———◆———

Q. The community of Brook became known for the manufacture of what type of cosmetic product?

A. Witch hazel lotion.

———◆———

Q. The supposed therapeutic abilities of local soil to relieve arthritis sufferers helped to bring recognition to what Warren County community?

A. Kramer.

———◆———

Q. Hoosier farms total how many acres of land?

A. 16,170,895.

———◆———

Q. In 1842, what was the going price for one-year-old steers in Indiana?

A. Five dollars each.

Q. While hiding from Indians in 1790, what cave system in southern Harrison County was discovered by Daniel Boone's brother?

A. Squire Boone Caverns.

———◆———

Q. What group taught farming to the Delaware, Kaskaskia, and Painkishawa Indians along White River in 1801?

A. Moravian missionaries.

———◆———

Q. Turner Physics Laboratory and Schertz Computer Center are both a part of what Indiana college campus?

A. Goshen College.

———◆———

Q. What type of ordnance was patented by Indianapolis resident Richard J. Gatling on November 4, 1862?

A. Rapid-fire machine gun (Gatling gun).

———◆———

Q. The General Assembly selected what rock as the state stone of Indiana in 1971?

A. Limestone.

———◆———

Q. What animal appears on the state seal of Indiana?

A. Buffalo.

———◆———

Q. In what Indiana city was the first diesel engine tractor assembled in May 1930?

A. Columbus.

Q. In 1853 Indiana's first natural-history collection was started by what institution of higher education?

A. Earlham College.

———◆———

Q. What is the approximate number of farms in Indiana?

A. 70,500.

———◆———

Q. 1884 was an all-time record high wheat production year for Indiana, with how many acres harvested?

A. 3,150,000.

———◆———

Q. What creature, named "Old Ben" and originally weighing 4,720 pounds, is preserved by taxidermy at Highland Park in Kokomo?

A. Hereford steer.

———◆———

Q. How deep are the glacial deposits in the buried Teays Valley area of central Indiana?

A. Up to 450 feet.

———◆———

Q. Portions of Hoosier National Forest may be found in how many counties?

A. Nine.

———◆———

Q. During Indiana's first oil and gas boom from 1886 to 1910, what was the most widely explored field?

A. The Trenton Field.

Q. During the Panic of 1893, hog prices dropped to what amount?

A. About three dollars per head.

———◆———

Q. The first gas refrigerator for home use was marketed in what Indiana city in 1926?

A. Evansville.

———◆———

Q. Approximately how many mink pelts were produced in Indiana in 1987?

A. 14,800.

———◆———

Q. In what Indiana city was the Dick test for scarlet fever developed?

A. Fort Wayne.

———◆———

Q. An automobile powered by an internal combustion gasoline engine, using a kerosene torch for ignition, was built by what Indianapolis resident in 1891?

A. Charles H. Black.

———◆———

Q. In 1987 what new record high was set for per acre yields of Indiana corn?

A. 135 bushels per acre.

———◆———

Q. What became the state flower of Indiana in 1957?

A. Peony.

Q. In what year did Indiana farmers produce the largest crop of oats ever?

A. 1928 (88,469,000 bushels).

———————◆———————

Q. Where is the Elkhart County 4-H and Agriculture Exposition held at the end of July?

A. East of Goshen.

———————◆———————

Q. How many covered bridges are in Parke County?

A. Thirty-four.

———————◆———————

Q. The first pneumatic rubber tire was developed in what Indiana city?

A. Kokomo.

———————◆———————

Q. Who gave the name of Pluto's Well to the main spring at French Lick?

A. Dr. Joseph G. Rogers.

———————◆———————

Q. What two lobes of the Ice Age Wisconsinan ice sheet most affected the formation of the Chain O' Lakes State Park?

A. The Saginaw and Erie Lobes.

———————◆———————

Q. On October 1, 1912, who became the first county agricultural agent in Indiana?

A. Leonard B. Clore.

Q. Situated in the vicinity of Mitchell, what is the largest number of sinkholes to be found within a single square mile?

A. 1,023.

———◆———

Q. What is the major cave in Versailles State Park?

A. Bat Cave.

———◆———

Q. How many pounds of tobacco were produced in Indiana during the record total production year of 1910?

A. 148,050,000.

———◆———

Q. In 1860, with Indiana leading all other states in number of hogs, what was the average number of hogs per Hoosier family?

A. Approximately ten.

———◆———

Q. What gas emanates from the springs of the French Lick area, creating a somewhat rotten-egg odor?

A. Hydrogen sulfide.

———◆———

Q. Who constructed Indiana's first blast furnace in 1834 to process native bog iron ore in the Mishawaka area?

A. Alanson M. Hurd.

———◆———

Q. What marsupial is found in Indiana?

A. The Virginia opossum.

Q. The sedimentary rocks from which the ridges, valleys, and hills of Brown County State Park are carved originated during what geologic period?

A. Mississippian.

Q. What major fault line exists in south-central Indiana?

A. Mt. Carmel Fault.

Q. In 1931 what tree was adopted by the General Assembly as the official state tree of Indiana?

A. Tulip tree (also called tulip poplar or yellow poplar).

Q. What natural amphitheater-like features created by the wind blowing off Lake Michigan may be seen at Indiana Dunes State Park?

A. Blowouts.

Q. In Madison, what attraction displays the facilities of a late 1800s medical practice?

A. Dr. William Hutchings Hospital.

Q. Plants and trees from around the world are featured at what Michigan City nature attraction in Pottawattomie Park?

A. International Friendship Gardens.

Q. What 88-acre tract of virgin timber has been preserved in Orange County?

A. Pioneer Mothers Memorial Forest.

Q. What price did Indiana wheat bring in 1900?

A. 69¢ per bushel.

———◆———

Q. What breed of dairy cattle was introduced into Indiana in 1878?

A. Guernsey.

———◆———

Q. Of what variety, are the two trees that appear on the right-hand portion of the state seal of Indiana?

A. Sycamore.

———◆———

Q. During what decade did soybeans first start to make inroads into the agricultural economy of Indiana?

A. 1920s.

———◆———

Q. Sandstone from the Mansfield Formation was once quarried in Indiana for the manufacture of what product?

A. Glass.

———◆———

Q. What are the two major waterfalls found in Shades State Park?

A. Silver Cascade and Maidenhair Falls.

———◆———

Q. A giant sycamore tree, measuring 43 feet, 3 inches in circumference at its base and 150 feet tall, stood in the early 1900s in the city park of what Greene County town?

A. Worthington.

Q. Martin County's richest iron ore, which may yield as much as sixty percent iron, is mostly made up of what mineral?

A. Goethite.

Q. What University of Notre Dame graduate discovered the process for creating synthetic rubber?

A. Father Nieuwland.

Q. In the 1820s what replaced the sickle as the main implement used by Indiana farmers to harvest wheat?

A. The grain cradle.

Q. Coal underlies approximately how many square miles of Indiana?

A. 6,500.

Q. How many types of trees grow in Indiana?

A. Over 130.

Q. Being utilized in Lawrence County by 1840, what was the first breed of draft horses used in the state?

A. Percheron.

Q. What mineral used for the manufacture of dry wall is mined from the St. Louis Limestone at Shoals?

A. Gypsum.

Q. The first successfully operated hatchery for what type of fish was opened near Martinsville in 1899?

A. Goldfish.

◆

Q. In what Indiana city was the nation's first "waterless" gas storage tank placed in service on February 10, 1925?

A. Michigan City.

◆

Q. What Indianapolis surgeon preformed the first gallstone operation on June 15, 1867?

A. Dr. J. S. Bobbs.

◆

Q. How many "victory gardens" were planted in Indianapolis during the first year of America's involvement in World War I?

A. Approximately 40,000.

◆

Q. What company built around 1840 southwest of Plymouth had one of Indiana's first Catalan style forges?

A. Plymouth Iron Works.

◆

Q. Hamer, Donaldson, Bronson, and Twin caves are all in what Indiana state park?

A. Spring Mill State Park.

◆

Q. Hoosier National Forest covers how many acres?

A. 188,000.

Q. What is the only variety of hummingbird found in Indiana?

A. Ruby-throated.

———◆———

Q. In the record total production year of 1965, how many tons of alfalfa hay were produced in Indiana?

A. 1,726,000.

———◆———

Q. Glenwood, Calumet, and Toleston are names of ancient beach lines of Lake Michigan, portions of which may be seen in what Indiana state park?

A. Indiana Dunes State Park.

———◆———

Q. In 1870 Switzerland and Floyd counties introduced the use of what new agriculture aid to Indiana?

A. Commercial fertilizer.

———◆———

Q. By what name are clay-rich, iron carbonate concretions from the Brownstown area called?

A. Clay ironstone.

———◆———

Q. How many work horses did Indiana have in 1914?

A. Appproximately 854,000.

———◆———

Q. In what Indiana state park is the Litten Natural Bridge found?

A. McCormicks Creek State Park.

Q. When was the peak number of approximately 800,000 milk cows reached in Indiana?

A. 1944–45.

———◆———

Q. Though not appropriated with funding by the State legislature until 1905, when was the Purdue Agricultural Experiment Station established?

A. July 1, 1887.

———◆———

Q. What area of Indiana is noted for its large quantities of geodes?

A. South-central.

———◆———

Q. A state fish hatchery for the rearing of bluegill, sunfish and bass is in what Lawrence County community?

A. Avoca.

———◆———

Q. What is the main stream that flows through Shades State Park?

A. Sugar Creek.

———◆———

Q. The quarry from which stone came for the construction of the Indiana State Capitol building is in what present-day state park?

A. McCormicks Creek State Park.

Q. 1872 brought the introduction of what breed of hogs into Indiana?

A. Yorkshire.

———◆———

Q. In what county does Lost River flow underground for several miles?

A. Orange.

———◆———

Q. What Indian earthwork at Vincennes was excavated by archeologist John Collett in 1873?

A. Sugar Loaf Mound.

———◆———

Q. What Alexandria resident first realized the possibilities of rock-wool in the late 1890s?

A. Charles C. Hill.

———◆———

Q. What metal used in spacecraft was developed in Kokomo?

A. Haynes Stellite.

———◆———

Q. Both Little Clifty Creek and Little Crooked Creek flow through what Indiana state park?

A. Clifty Falls State Park.

———◆———

Q. What southwestern Lawrence County natural attraction ranks as one of the world's ten largest cave systems?

A. Bluespring Caverns.

Q. What automotive accessory was first offered to the public in Anderson on January 25, 1952?

A. The automatic headlight dimmer (Autronic-Eye).

Q. On Indian Creek, some ten miles southwest of Bloomington, what company fired up Indiana's second blast furnace in 1839?

A. Randolph Ross & Sons Virgina Iron Works.

Q. What is the largest type of owl found in Indiana?

A. Great horned owl.

Q. What Indiana state park near Anderson features a large ancient earthwork, nine feet high and almost one-fourth mile in circumference?

A. Mounds State Park.

Q. What type of canned juice was first produced in Kokomo?

A. Tomato.

Q. What is Indiana's largest state park?

A. Brown County State Park (15,543 acres).

Q. What 684-acre nature area, sponsored by the Indiana Audubon Society, is in Fayette County?

A. Mary Grey Bird Sanctuary.

Q. What is Indiana's most valuable mineral resource?

A. Bituminous coal.

◆

Q. Forests cover approximately how many acres in Indiana?

A. Four million.

◆

Q. Sociologists Robert S. and Helen Merrell Lynd conducted a five-year study of what Indiana town, with their findings being published in 1929 in a book entitled *Middletown*?

A. Muncie.

◆

Q. What noted scientist, called the "Father of American Geology," came to New Harmony in 1826?

A. William Maclure.

◆

Q. What mineral found in the Alexandria area is essential in the manufacture of rock-wool?

A. Argillaceous limestone.

◆

Q. Lake James and Snow Lake may be enjoyed in what Indiana state park?

A. Pokagon State Park.

◆

Q. What is the best known of Indiana's building stones?

A. Salem Limestone.

Q. What famous rose was developed in New Castle?

A. American Beauty.

---◆---

Q. Franklin and Union counties share what long, narrow reservoir?

A. Brookville Lake.

---◆---

Q. What 900-acre nature area is managed by Goshen College?

A. Mary Lee Environmental Learning Center.

---◆---

Q. Indiana opened what new state park on January 9, 1988?

A. Summit Lake State Park.

---◆---

Q. What is the circumference of a giant hollow sycamore stump on display at Highland Park, in Kokomo?

A. Fifty-one feet.

---◆---

Q. In 1875 Clark and Dubois counties became the first in Indiana to apply what substance to highly acid farmland?

A. Lime.

---◆---

Q. What frontier garden in Madison features plants originally brought from Virginia around 1820?

A. Talbot-Hyatt Pioneer Garden.

Q. What education and wildlife facility is situated near Battle Ground?

A. Wolf Park.

Q. The Mixsawbah State Fish Hatchery is adjacent to what fish and wildlife area?

A. Kingsbury State Fish and Wildlife Area.

Q. Who was commissioned in 1837 to conduct a preliminary geological survey of Indiana?

A. David Dale Owen.

Q. The chilled-steel plow was invented by what South Bend resident in 1868?

A. James Oliver.

Q. In a 1940 Indiana agricultural competition, what was the winning yield for a two-acre test plot of soybeans?

A. Forty-three bushels per acre.

Q. At the peak of production in 1926, how many mines were operating in the Bicknell coal field?

A. Fourteen.

Q. What state park was named for the large flocks of wild turkeys common in the area during early pioneer days?

A. Turkey Run State Park.

Q. In 1836 the mineral springs of what area became the first to be commercialized?

A. French Lick.

◆

Q. What large reservor southeast of Bloomington was a joint project of the Indiana Department of Resources and the U.S. Corps of Engineers?

A. Lake Monroe.

◆

Q. A team of Purdue University scientists developed what type of equipment to detect tiny insects hidden inside seeds?

A. Ultrasonic listening device.

◆

Q. What is the largest museum for children in the world?

A. The Indianapolis Children's Museum.

◆

Q. Where was the first successful automatic telephone system installed in 1892?

A. La Porte.

◆

Q. What unusual geological formation overlooks the bottom lands along White River near Worthington?

A. Devil's Tea Table Rock.

◆

Q. What is the largest farm organization in Indiana?

A. Indiana Farm Bureau.

Q. What "popcorn czar" earned a bachelor's degree in agriculture from Purdue in 1928 and some sixty years later was given an honorary doctoral degree by the university?

A. Orville Redenbacher.

———◆———

Q. Other than appleseeds, Johnny Appleseed planted what kinds of seeds to aid pioneer families?

A. Herbs (for medical remedies).

———◆———

Q. What 1,710-acre state park is in Union County?

A. Whitewater State Park.

———◆———

Q. What Indiana town served as headquarters of the United State Geological Survey for seventeen years?

A. New Harmony.

———◆———

Q. What nature facility northeast of Lafayette features fourteen acres of rugged glacier-made ridges, with native trees and wild flowers?

A. Clegg Botanical Garden.

———◆———

Q. The first Studebaker automobiles were powered by what type of energy?

A. Electricity.